Mollie
is *Three*

Mollie is *Three*

Growing Up in School

Vivian Gussin Paley

The University of Chicago Press
Chicago and London

The University of Chicago Press, Chicago 60637
The University of Chicago Press, Ltd., London
© 1986 by The University of Chicago
All rights reserved. Published 1986
Paperback edition 1988
Printed in the United States of America

09 08 07 06 05   7 8 9 10

Library of Congress Cataloging-in-Publication Data

Paley, Vivian Gussin, 1929–
    Mollie is three.
    1. Child development—United Sates—Case studies.
2. Fantasy in children—Case studies. 3. Play—Case
studies. 4. Paley, Vivian Gussin, 1929– 5. Nursery
school teachers—United States—Biography. I. Title.
II. Title: Molly is three.
LB117.P235   1986   305.2'33   85-24589
ISBN: 0-226-64494-4 (paper)

Contents

In memory of
Ida and William Palevsky

Foreword

Mollie is Three describes a year in the life of a little girl
and her classmates in a nursery school classroom organized
by Vivian Paley, one of the most talented students of the
teaching-learning process writing today. An unusual con-
fluence of social and scientific factors make this work especially relevant to students of human development and educational practice.

During its short history in the United States, academic
research on child development, like other branches of the
behavioral sciences, has been preoccupied with problems of
scientific methodology. If one samples any of the leading
journals in the field, it soon becomes clear that quantitative
methods, preferably quantification based upon experimental manipulations, are the major source of evidence about
the processes that propel children's development. The vir-
tues of such an approach are clear. Quantification and experimental control provide an objective data base which can
be used to warrant causal claims about the factors that ac-
celerate and retard development.

At the same time, the application of experimental tech-
niques to the explanation of, and prediction of, human behavior also suffers from a number of acknowledged short-
comings. For purposes of the present discussion, two
difficulties are most serious. First, as Walker Percy wryly
comments, "There is a secret about the scientific method
which every scientist knows and takes as a matter of
course, but which the layman does not know . . . The secret
is this: Science cannot utter a single word about the individual molecule, thing, or creature in so far as it is an individual but only in so far as it is like other individuals" (*The
Message in the Bottle*). Applied to psychology, the discipline
which studies *individual* behavior and consciousness, this

limitation on the scientific method is particularly disheartening.

Second, it is an accepted truth that development is not an instantaneous process; it occurs over time, which means that time must be taken to allow the dynamics of the process to reveal themselves. Yet most experimentation (and most observations of children for that matter) involves only very brief time samples, owing to problems of cost and practicality, among others.

These limitations of experimental methodology are, of course, old news to psychologists and educators who have had to resolve the contradictions in educational practice that arise because the abstract child that emerges from experimental-quantitative methods is difficult to reconcile with the flesh-and-blood children who confront the teacher, therapist, or social worker (to say nothing of the parents) in real life. Recent decades have witnessed a variety of suggestions on ways to escape from the limitations of existing psychological science without abandoning its goals.

In the world's most famous program of research on child development, Jean Piaget ignored the canons of proper psychological research when he substituted observation and clinical interviews with individual children (including his own) for averaged data from large groups of children and formal procedures of data collection. So marked was Piaget's departure from standard methodologies that during the 1940s and 1950s, when developmental psychology was beginning to blossom in the United States, his work could be (and was) almost totally ignored. Even now, in the mid 1980s, when Piaget's work has been rediscovered and lionized for two decades, his methods are widely considered too unsystematic and informal for proper scientific use. As a result, a small industry has been devoted to replicating his observations and evaluating his claims using standardized versions of his famous tests and appropriately large samples of children.

A second alternative to American-style psychological experimentation and quantification that came to prominence at about the same time as Piaget's ideas began to attract widespread attention was the effort of ethologists to reveal basic laws of behavior by observing animals in their natural habits so thoroughly that the invariant organizing principles of behavior would reveal themselves through the flux of specific behaviors. Experiments, according to the ethologist's way of proceeding, were useful primarily in the form of small impediments inserted into the stream of behavior which revealed the processes underlying behavior in the course of disrupting it.

Common to all of these approaches is a desire to lay bare the universal bases of development as a precondition for making sense of everyday experience. Each methodology rests on a set of procedures which allows its creator to claim that children (or animals) of such-and-such an age behave in such-and-such a way because of their genetic constitution and universal aspects of the environment.

If, instead of occupying the role of analyst-theorist who stood apart from the creature being studied, one is responsible for guiding the development of individual children as a professional commitment (for example, if one happens to be a nursery school teacher), the normative generalizations of analytic science, while certainly interesting and suggestive, may appear inappropriately abstract. Reduced from the level of universal generalization to the concrete realities of twenty-four small children who must be productively occupied in a relatively small space for several hours a day, the teacher of preschool children can be forgiven for focusing below the level of grand abstraction. Following Goethe she may declare, "Grey is every theory, evergreen the tree of life."

At the same time, the preschool teacher is in a unique position to resolve some of the very issues left unresolved by others who study children and their development. Should she wish to do so (we use the feminine pronoun in this case because it is a "she" we are writing about), she can combine the observational/intervention strategy favored by the ethologist with the participant observation methods of the anthropologist. Present from the time children first enter the classroom until they graduate to their next educational institution, she is in a perfect position to trace development across long stretches of time and a broad range of specific contexts. If she is well read in theories of development and instruction, and well supplied with human empathy, the result can be a rare blend of science and humanism.

Mollie is Three is the fourth in a series of monographs about learning and development among preschool children published by Vivian Paley since 1979. Each study represents a stage in the evolution of her methodology and an exploration of a different aspect of the role of teaching-learning experiences in human development—hers and the children's.

In her first book, *White Teacher,* we encounter Mrs. Paley at an important transition point in her own development as a teacher. After many years of teaching she has come to Chicago at a time when racial tension is severe and she is uncertain of her own role as a white teacher whose students include many black children. The focal point of this first book is the jumping off point for those to follow, for in it Mrs. Paley learns how to find common ground between herself and the children across enormous gulfs of age and culture. Stories and play are an essential element of that common ground, but the eventual place they will play in her work is subordinated to the sociopolitical drama of events outside the classroom.

As a part of the experiences that are chronicled in *White Teacher,* Mrs. Paley's ability to listen carefully and respectfully to what her small charges are trying to mean led her to the crucial discovery of a methodology especially appropriate to the study of preschool development. Eventually it also led to the publication of *Wally's Stories.* Like many teachers before her, Mrs. Paley had made storytelling a regular part of her classroom. She had also encouraged children to dictate their own stories to her. But, with few exceptions, the opportunities to create stories were only occasionally taken up by the children, and then usually by girls.

One day, when Wally had spent two periods on a "time out" chair because he could not keep himself out of trouble, Mrs. Paley, hoping to distract him from himself, asked if he would like to write a story. Wally was surprised. "You didn't teach me how to write yet," he said. "You just tell me the story, Wally. I'll write the words," Mrs. Paley replied. Wally told a story about a troublemaking dinosaur who destroyed a city and was put in jail. "Is that the end?" Mrs. Paley asked. "He promised to be good so they let him go home and his mother was waiting," Wally added.

Up to this point, the anecdote could have been repeated in any number of kindergartens or nursery schools, but Mrs. Paley, feeling sorry for Wally, sought to please him by allowing him to act out the story and to include other children in the performance. She reports:

> It made Wally very happy, and a flurry of story writing began that continued and grew all year. The boys dictated as many stories as the girls, and we acted out each story the day it was written if we could.
>
> Before, we had never acted out these stories. We had dramatized every other kind of printed word— fairy tales, story books, poems, songs—but it had always seemed enough just to write the children's words. Obviously it was not; the words did not sufficiently represent the action, which needed to be shared. For this alone, the children would give up play time, as it was a true extension of play.

This "true extension of play" provided the perfect middle ground between Mrs. Paley and the children. Many psychologists had focused on preschoolers' play as the most representative form of their activity in which the special features of their way of thinking is most clearly expressed. Like play, the structure and content of the children's dramatizations were under their own control. But, unlike play, their scripted performances were not entirely spontaneous and subject to change; the children's play selves had been fictionalized again. The fleeting impulse had been caught

in flight. It could now be savored, improved upon, and con-
tributed to by people who were not present at its inception.
During dramatization, Mrs. Paley had a legitimate and re-
spected role of director and commentator, an amanuensis of
development.

Having arrived at an especially revealing way to study
and guide preschoolers' development, Mrs. Paley first applied her new methods to the study of early sex role so-
cialization in *Boys and Girls*. Like *White Teacher, Boys and
Girls* treats an issue of widespread and pressing social concern; like *Wally's Stories* it uses a combination of story gen-
erating, observation, pretend play, and discussions with the
children to construct a picture of the children's thoughts
and actions.

With *Mollie* we arrive at the central issue: the process of
development itself.

In the pages that follow, the reader will accompany Mollie through her first year of nursery school. We meet her on
the first day of school, just before her third birthday; we
take leave of her, already an "oldtimer" as she approaches
her fourth. In the beginning, paradox and perplexity are
prominent features of Mollie's experience as a child and our
own experience as readers. Her actions appear only margin-
ally related to her words. We, like she, are uncertain of our
surroundings.

Day by day, event by event, page by page, patterns
emerge and cumulate. Yet as we read about Mollie's experience and her interpretations of it, we can never be quite
certain when she has made a significant developmental
step. Apparent moments of progress toward clarity and understanding come and go, sometimes within a single conversation or play episode.

To generations of developmental psychologists and educators brought up on theories of preschool development arrived at by short-term observation, coding schemes, experiments, and statistical verification procedures, there are
many surprises in store as Mollie's development is traced
through the classroom events of her fourth year.

In place of an idealized, generalized child, Vivian Paley presents us with a picture of the formation of human consciousness that provides a flesh-and-blood representation of William James's intuition about human consciousness at all stages and the process by which we all wrest pattern from the flux of experience. We can say of Mollie, as James said of history, that her world

> is full of partial stories that run parallel to one another, beginning and ending at odd times. They mutually interlace and interfere at points but we cannot unite them completely in our minds . . . It is easy to see the world's history pluralistically, as a rope of which each fiber tells a separate tale; but to conceive of each cross-section of the rope as an absolutely single fact, and to sum the whole longitudinal series into one being living an undivided life, is harder . . . The great world's ingredients, so far as they are beings, seem, like the rope's fibres, to be discontinuous, crosswise, and to cohere only in the longitudinal direction.

And so it is with Mollie, three years old and growing up in school with some help from her friends and teachers, among whom she is lucky to count Vivian Paley.

MICHAEL COLE

Preface

If, in the world of fantasy play, four- and five-year-olds may be called characters in search of a plot, then the three-year-old is surely a character in search of a character.

Place this three-year-old in a room with other threes, and sooner or later they will become an acting company. Should there happen to be a number of somewhat older peers about to offer stage directions and dialogue, the metamorphosis will come sooner rather than later. The dramatic images that flutter through their minds, as so many unbound stream-of-consciousness novels, begin to emerge as audible scripts to be performed on demand.

The characters and plots are there, waiting, always in the process of becoming. Even when the teacher is unaware of the fantasy, the children are certain it is there. For this reason they watch one another more closely than ever they would watch me, the teacher, for I cannot teach them the subject they most wish to learn. And since the subject I most wish to learn is the children, I must concentrate on this play, for they will teach me who they are by the fantasies they explore.

Why is fantasy play the most compelling attraction in the preschool curriculum? Some would say it *is* the curriculum. "In play," the Russian psychologist Lev Vygotsky tells us, "a child is above his average age, above his daily behavior; in play it is as though he were a head taller than himself."

Mollie is three, and eager to grow a head taller. Not knowing what to expect, she responds to those who appear to fulfill the promise of her fantasies. Serious voices filter through the blur of confusing purposes, saying: Watch me, I am different. Pretend that you too are in another form, doing other things, feeling fearless or afraid, big or small, far away or as near as the kitchen table.

Mollie listens, and, as she learns to pretend that school is something else, it begins to make sense. The fantasies form a common thread connecting people and ideas, materials and phrases, private thoughts and public events. Her pathway to reality leads through the doll corner, the building blocks, and the story table. I try to stand aside and allow Mollie and her classmates to speak for themselves.

It is not easy to wait and listen. In my haste to display the real world, I offer the children solutions to unimagined problems. My neatly classified bits and pieces clamor for attention, but the boys and girls seek connections with one another and follow their instincts into play. It is this view of growing up I write about, and, if it sometimes has the look of unfocused experimental theater, then the picture is accurate. The children and their inventions do not submit well to explanations and labels, but their words, which I capture daily with an ever ready tape recorder, tell a story filled with mystery and drama.

"When I get four, I'll be three," Mollie says shortly before her third birthday and, a few months later, revising her sights, she tells Erik, "You know what? When I'm four I'm going to be five like Maria."

She knows something big is about to happen and she is right. The reader may need to wait a while, as I must, to gain the measure of her growth (briefly alluded to in the Epilogue), but for Mollie the way is immediately available: it is called fantasy play.

1

On the first day, Mollie sits quietly at the playdough table watching Fredrick. She is waiting to find out what happens in school, and he is someone who makes things happen. He wants to know why he is here and how he can impose himself on so many people. He begins in unsubtle ways, knocking over blocks, grabbing toys, stomping on dolls, throwing sand—the list is familiar.

The other three-year-olds may have committed similar mischief, but seldom in such rapid succession and not yet in a classroom. Fredrick exaggerates and speeds up these behaviors, forcing me to reveal my intentions.

"Why do you bother everyone, Fredrick?"

"Don't talk to me! I hate this school!"

"I must talk to you. I'm your teacher."

"The next day after this one, I'm never coming back."

"But it's your class. You have to come back."

"Then I'm angry."

He shows me he is angry by turning his back when I read "Curious George," but at dismissal time he sits on my lap.

"Am I bigger than everyone on this porch?" he asks.

"No, you're not," I tell him. "The four-year-olds are bigger and so are the teachers." There are thirteen fours in our class, most of whom were here last year.

"No, I'm the biggest. And the strongest."

The next morning he snatches the entire supply of playdough from Mollie, Emily, and Stuart. "It's mine!" he shouts defiantly.

"Give it back, Fredrick. You can't grab things from people."

"It's mine."

"They had it first."

"I don't have any."

"You have to say, 'Can I have some?' "

"No."

He cannot wait for such amenities. Nor has he reason to believe that the children will hand over a portion of their playdough; he certainly would not. Since others may have the same possessive urge, he'd better act out the feeling first.

Mollie's eyes follow Fredrick as he confronts the unknown, ordered world of the classroom. She sits across from him at the snack table when he talks about the wicked monsters who enter his room at night.

"Last night I saw a monster in my bed—a big white monster. Then a dinosaur." He looks around, expecting encouragement.

"Then what did the dinosaur do?" Stuart asks.

"He hided downstairs. Then he went upstairs." Fredrick pauses to eat his graham cracker, watching me.

"It was a dream, Fredrick," I say.

"No, teacher, listen, I want to tell you something. I saw a big white monster and then I saw a dinosaur and it was hiding by my bed under the covers and it was a monster in my room."

"Fredrick, I know it really seemed like the monster was in your room, but it was all in your dream."

"It wasn't a dream. So I left the door open and then the dinosaur came in and then he didn't eat me this time. He was putting his arm like this. With his fingers. He wanted to eat me up because he didn't want me to go to school."

"Why not?"

"Because he wanted to eat me all up so I couldn't go to school. Because I wanted to come to school. And he wouldn't let me."

"I'm glad you came, Fredrick."

"And it wasn't a dream. There was a really monster."

"It might have been a shadow on the wall, in the dark, shaped like a monster."

"No."

The children at the table look as if they too have seen these monsters. Mollie asks, "Is it the kind with green on top?" Fredrick nods. "Also on the bottom," he adds.

It is the first time Mollie has spoken directly to another child. She talks to me early in the morning, before the others come, but grows silent as the classroom fills with children.

Fredrick has ways of getting immediate responses from people. Today he makes Mollie cry, and Libby, a four-year-old, is indignant. "That boy took the little girl's cash register," she reports to me.

"Give it back, Fredrick," I order. "Mollie is crying. You can have it when she's finished."

Anger makes Mollie eloquent. "I'm already going to be finished now," she sobs.

"Do you mean you *are* finished now, Mollie?"

She tightens her grip. "No! Not yet now!"

"Okay. She'll be finished in a little while, Fredrick. Then you can have your turn."

"Turns" and "little whiles" mean nothing to Fredrick. In five minutes he is back, sitting on the cash register, and Mollie is crying again.

This time, Libby takes charge. "He's a bad boy! Don't let him come to your birthday. He's just a robber."

Mollie stops crying and stares at Libby. Fredrick also pauses to consider. "Yeah, I *am* a robber," he says solemnly.

"Well, too bad for you," Libby counters, haughtily. "Because robbers can't come in the doll corner, ha, ha, ha!" She looks at me for confirmation. Libby is in the group who decided last year that robbers are not allowed wherever babies are sleeping.

"She's right, Fredrick. If you want to play in the doll corner, you'll have to be something else, not a robber."

"He can be the father," Samantha says. "Put on this vest, Fredrick."

"Mollie is the baby," Libby decides. "Lie down here, sweet child."

Suddenly, Mollie and Fredrick are part of a drama that has its own conventions. The roles are assigned, and, for the duration of the plot, events will be governed by an evolving set of rules that reflects the children's own logic. There

3

is nothing in my curriculum that can match the doll corner in its potential for examining behavior and judging the aftermath. The two three-year-olds know intuitively that once they begin to pretend they become accountable to the community of pretenders.

2

Mollie is brought to school every day before eight. In the empty rooms, her large vocabulary pours out in search of time and place.

"I'm not too big to reach that," she says, trying to hang up her jacket. "But my already birthday is going to come now. Then I can be big to reach it."

"When is your birthday, Mollie?"

"Tomorrow. It's called October ninth."

"October is the next month after this one. Then you'll be three, Mollie. This month is called September."

"When I get four, I'll be three."

She joins me at the painting table as I prepare the art materials. "Can you put in the brushes, Mollie?"

"I *can* put in the brushes." She inserts one brush in a jar of red paint and begins to cover the paper in front of her.

"The other jars need brushes too, Mollie."

"They *do* need brushes too," she echoes, without looking up.

"Or do you want me to put them in?" I suggest, a bit impatiently.

"Do you want . . . do I *not* . . . I do *not* want you," she answers.

Mollie is a passionate grammarian, reconstructing my sentences into useful shapes. She cares about form but eschews the message. Her obligation is fulfilled once she creates a sentence. In effect, she has pretend conversations with me.

4

"This pie is for Daddy," Mollie murmurs, taking up a piece of playdough at the next table. She pounds and flattens the soft, floury mass, punctuating her monologue. "Daddy wants to finish dinner when he gets dinner and go to work and work some work. Give me a big piece a little tiny piece . . . "

"Look, Mollie, I made a snake."

She examines my face, as if trying to understand the context of my remark. "Is that a real one? A real snake *that* one is. This is my castle. This."

"Can my snake live in your castle?"

"I'm going to roll him up when he's sleeping. Sh-sh. Time to go to school, little baby snake. Put on your school clothes."

As the fantasy develops, her sentences achieve a continuity that eludes our conversations. She has moved to another plane and can suddenly view an entire scene about to unfold.

"I'm the mommy snake. 'Read me a book,' says the baby snake." Mollie turns invisible pages, pretending to read. "The horsie and the chicken. And the robbers. Once upon a time there lived a horse and a chicken and a dog. And the next morning there was a robber in the house. That's Fredrick. He's the robber. That was scary."

"The robber is scary?"

"The horsie and the chicken."

Fredrick is the first classmate to enter Mollie's early morning talk. She examines his behavior inside another fantasy and does not feel threatened; he scares the horse and chicken, not Mollie. Fredrick is an actor in her story and he knows "the monster with green on top" who visits her at night. If she continues to watch him, he may help her disclose other secrets not yet put into words.

3

Mollie tells me no secrets, but she is full of information. "Red is my favorite color," she says.

"I do notice you paint a lot of red pictures."

"Yes, I *do* notice a lot of red pictures that you do notice." She halts, then completes the thought. "That I paint."

Now, along with red paint, she institutes another ritual: she moves to a new chair for each painting. "Green is my favorite color, orange is my favorite color, blue is my favorite green." But she continues to use only red.

"Mollie, it's best to stay in the same seat and just get another sheet of paper. You're using up every piece on the table. The other children won't have a place to paint when they come."

"They want the playdough."

"Here's a better idea. When you finish a picture, pick it up like this and put it on the rack to dry. Watch me. Then take another piece, go back to the same chair . . . "

"To the same chair," Mollie says, moving over.

"Mollie, you're not watching. Look. Up goes my paper, now another paper, paint, paint, paint, up it goes on the rack, then another paper, now back to the same chair."

She stares at my hasty swirls of color traveling back and forth, but has stopped listening. As the room fills with children, I give my seat to Adam, a four-year-old, who covers his paper with graceful arcs of every color. Suddenly he drops his brush and jumps up.

"Hey, Tulio! Whadya bring? Hey, lemme see!" He runs off, leaving a wet brush on his unfinished rainbow. By the time I return, Fredrick has wiped a fistful of brushes across Adam's painting and the surrounding newspaper.

In the space of an hour, Mollie has observed a number of painting behaviors, including mine. She repeats my words, but they seem to carry little more meaning than her singsong recitation of favorite colors. It is Fredrick's technique she thinks about the next day.

"Fredrick doesn't know how to do it," Mollie states. " He has to use too many colors. Red is his favorite color."

When Fredrick comes to the painting table, I mention Mollie's concern. "Mollie thinks you use too many colors."

"What?"

"Mollie. This is Mollie. She's at your snack table. She thinks you should paint a red picture."

"Huh? Oh. Is this red?" He lifts the red brush and drippingly moves it back and forth on a paper.

"Here. She can have it."

Mollie accepts the gift without looking at Fredrick and hangs it on the drying rack. She sees the rules and regulations of the painting table, not through my words, but in the actions of other children. Fredrick has, in a sense, *pretended* to paint a red picture, and Mollie can now act out the procedure of painting and drying. But I was also pretending; that is, demonstrating. Why didn't my example suffice? Apparently my pretending does not carry the vision she needs in order to understand the meaning of an event.

My lesson is a set of rules without tangible evidence or dramatic context. It offers Mollie no opportunity to imagine herself playing a role in relation to another child. She cannot step up to that elevated perch from which to see the whole picture.

4

Repetition of little memorized behaviors is the three-year-old's specialty, erupting into new insights according to unseen schedules and fooling the adult into premature expectations.

Mollie, for example, calls off numerals in fast succession, as if really counting. She tells me the number of brushes – one to fifteen – while I line them up in paint jars. In her rapid calculations, she misses a few brushes at the start and adds a few at the end.

We play "math" games at the playdough table that inevitably conform to her rules.

"Make me a bird's nest" is the way she begins one of her games.

"How many eggs does the mother bird lay?" I must then ask, molding a nest out of playdough. I cannot vary my words or actions; the game is to proceed as originally played.

"Six only," she says.

"Here they are. Plop, plop, plop, plop, plop, plop. How many eggs, Mollie?"

"One, two, three!" She holds her fingers over two eggs at a time. I have already learned that if I correct her and ask her to count again, I am spoiling the game.

I gather up the six eggs and press them together. "Now how many does the mother lay?"

"Three only three."

"Very well. Plop, plop, plop."

"One, two, three, four, five!" For the remainder of today's game, she counts to five no matter how many eggs are in the nest. There is no necessary connection between eggs and the words called numbers, though I notice that she assembles her four snack crackers daily without error.

Margaret arrives, bursting with news. She is also three, but older than Mollie by several months. "Blue and yellow is green," she says, raising her eyebrows importantly. "My mother showed me."

"We could try to make green," I suggest.

"Blue and yellow is green already."

"I know, but let's see if we can do it. Which paint shall we use first?"

"Red."

"Red? Well, you said blue, so let's start with blue. Then you said yellow. There. Now mix it up. What color is it?"

"Green!"

"Green, green, a shame to be seen," Mollie sings, borrowing a line from "Jennie Jenkins."

"So, how did we make green, Margaret?"

"It commed out of yellow. First yellow, then red."

"Red? Did we use red?"

"Then green."

The next morning, Mollie tells me green is her favorite color. "Do you remember how we made green, Mollie?"

"Yes. I *do* remember. Mommy made it. With a spoon you do it. That's how it works."

"Can you do it?"

"Yes, I can." She picks up several brushes. "This is going in yellow. This is going in red. This is going in magenta. Somebody will paint on this side. I will *not* change my seat."

"Watch me, Mollie. I'm making green. First a blue spot. Then what color?"

"Red."

"Okay, we'll put red on the blue. Does it turn into green?"

"Yes, it does turn into green. Green is my favorite color."

"Mollie, you know this isn't green. It's purple."

"I *know* this isn't green."

The lesson is over for Mollie, but not for me. How many of my lessons and rules add up to "blue and yellow is green"? And how often do preferred behaviors amount to "green is my favorite color"? Mollie's method of painting is as far from my expectations as is Fredrick's, yet I label one idiosyncratic and the other chaotic. Fredrick uses every brush he can reach, Mollie restricts herself to one color; he covers the newspaper, she moves around the table. She is "funny," he is "negative."

Later, Fredrick slumps across from me at the painting table. He has been sharply reprimanded by my assistant, Mrs. Alter, and he wants to show me his anger. He reaches for the brushes with both hands, expecting to be stopped.

"I changed my mind about your painting, Fredrick."

"Why?"

"Because I can see that the way you paint is faster. So, if you want to use a lot of brushes at once, it's all right, but use just one set of jars, so the others stay clean. And, also, when you're finished, wash your brushes so the next person will have clean ones to use."

Fredrick's face lights up at the thought of washing dirty brushes. He paints a quick design, then takes six brushes into the bathroom. Five minutes later he emerges wet and smiling with reasonably clean brushes and replaces them carefully in the paint jars. The procedure makes sense; we started with *his* thinking instead of my rule.

Libby accomplishes the same thing in the doll corner. She accepts Fredrick as a robber and goes on from there. Why not? Everything in the doll corner is make-believe. If you can be a baby, you can be a robber, and, when babies sleep, robbers rob elsewhere.

But where? Am I to pretend Fredrick is a "pretend robber" every time he grabs the playdough? By what rule of fantasy do robbers refrain from stealing playdough?

My analysis is held in check by a loud wail coming from the block area. Fredrick is on the floor crying furiously.

"He did it on purpose!" Erik yells. "For no reason. He knocked the whole ship over!"

"I see that, Erik. But I don't want you to push him down."

"I told him. I grabbed him to stop!"

Libby's doll-corner logic comes to my aid. "Who are you pretending to be, Fredrick?"

My question surprises him. He didn't realize he was pretending. "I don't know," he sobs.

"Erik, who are *you* supposed to be?"

"I'm Luke."

"Fredrick doesn't know who to be."

Erik gives Fredrick a serious look. "Do you want to be a bad guy or a good guy?"

"A good guy."

"Then you can be Han Solo. But he can't play with us. We're too busy."

"Fredrick and I will just watch for a while," I suggest, but Fredrick has other ideas. He runs to the sand table and pokes his arm through Maria's sand castle. I am too angry to ask who he is pretending to be.

"Are you going to spank him?" Maria asks.

"We don't spank. We tell the rules over and over until people remember. They have to remember without being punished." My voice sounds punitive.

"I hate this place!" Fredrick shouts. "And you don't like me."

When I am angry, he tells me I don't like him. At this moment I do prize Maria's sand castle more than I like Fredrick. He hangs his head and stares at the floor; there is no energy left to think about reasonable solutions. Anger has the same effect on me.

At the snack table, Christopher asks me, "Are you mad at Fredrick?"

"No. Not any more."

Christopher is the newest three-year-old, having joined our class two weeks after the others. We hardly know him, but Erik already calls him a "troublemaker."

"Why aren't you mad?" Christopher asks.

"Because, because," Mollie states slowly. "Because now Fredrick is nice."

"And before?" I ask.

"That's because he was a robber." Fredrick, she knows, plays many different roles. She can better explain his behavior as a character portrayal than in terms of classroom rules.

5

Fredrick wants to dictate a story. He has been listening to the older children and has watched me write their words on lined paper. When it is his turn, he says, "Fredrick." I print his name at the top of the page and wait.

"Fredrick," he repeats.

"What do you do in the story?"

"Nothing."

"You could go to school."

"No."

"Just 'Fredrick'?"

"Yes."

At the end of the morning we go upstairs to the carpeted piano room where we sing and act out the stories told each day during playtime. I hold up Fredrick's page and read, "Fredrick." He runs to the center of the rug and smiles. The others, seated on low benches against the walls, smile back but I yield to the teacher's role.

"Is anything different about Fredrick's story?" I ask.

"Because he's Fredrick," Libby answers.

"Right. But I wondered about a story that has only one word."

John, nearly five, responds quickly. "It's not one word. It's one person."

Of course. A person *is* a story. Fredrick need not do something to justify his presence in the story.

The children accept other ideas Fredrick has that I challenge. He frequently falls off the bench in the piano room and rolls on the rug when the singing or story-acting go on too long. Sometimes he pulls Stuart down with him.

"You're spoiling people's stories," I tell him, though a casual glance around the room disproves my statement. The tumbling, in fact, seems to provide needed relief. Mollie watches Fredrick and Stuart with more interest than she gives to the stories. She especially turns to them when there is a monster on stage.

In the morning, Fredrick waits for me at the story table. Mollie sits next to him, coloring with a red crayon. "Here's a crayon, Fredrick," she says.

"I don't want it."

"What are you doing?"

"Telling a story."

The moment I appear, he says, "Fredrick."

"Why don't you tell about the dinosaur that came into your room?" I prompt.

"That didn't happen in my story." He speaks as if the story is already written.

"Hm-m. Let's see if I can help. Is Stuart in the story?"

"Yes."

"Okay. Fredrick and Stuart. What are they doing?"

"Something."

"In the playground?"

"No."

"Falling off the bench?"

"That *did* happen in my story!" He eyes are shining. "First Fredrick falled off the bench," he says, "then Stuart falled off."

Upstairs, I read, "First Fredrick falled off the bench, then Stuart falled off."

The children beam at the inescapable rightness of the sentence. It is indeed Fredrick's story; no one else could have told it. When he and Stuart reenact their roles, I am struck by the appropriateness of it all. How odd that I supply this line for his story, the very action I disapproved of earlier. Fredrick has forced me to recognize the validity of falling off a bench, just as earlier I had to admit there is no sensible objection to using six brushes at once if you wash them afterwards.

Since Fredrick so often makes me distinguish between convenience and logic, Mollie is wise to monitor his activities. She also has begun to watch the children whom *he* watches. "What are you doing?" she asks them. Those she questions are usually the nonconformists, the children who are passionately devoted to self-determined goals. They are the ones, in particular, who continually reorganize the classroom into fantasy worlds that lie outside my jurisdiction.

6

Fredrick shadows Erik and John, hoping to enter their magical sphere. He calls them "the big boys" and waits quietly in the music room for their stories to be acted out. They are ardent storytellers, faithfully extending their good guy–bad guy play to the printed page. "Put me on the story list," they say nearly every morning, referring to the sign-up sheet that formalizes the day's dramatic fare. Today, John tells a "Knight Riders" story.

"Once upon a time there was a black horse that was a good guy and a red horse that was a bad guy. Then we were running away to steal things and two Knight Riders tried to stop us but they couldn't."

Surprisingly, it is Mollie, not Fredrick, who copies John's story. I would have expected her to be moved by the kind of story Amelia tells:

"Once there was two sisters called Wonderwoman and the other one was called Cinderella and they went to the beach and then they played and then they had their supper."

Mollie prefers, however, to talk about bad guys and horses.

"Tell me a story," she says. "On the list."

"Do *you* want to tell the story, Mollie? Shall I put your name on the story list?"

"Tell me a story about a bad guy and a horse. The robbers and the horse."

"What do the robbers do?" I ask.

"He takes things away from the girl."

"When we act out your story, will you be the girl?"

Mollie shakes her head. "It's too scary for people. It's too scary for Fredrick," she says.

The next day, Mollie expands her theme. "It's about a bad guy and a red horse. A ghost story. About a bad guy. Sometimes it's scary and sometimes it's Knight Rider. I'm Knight Rider. A ghost. It's not a mama and not a baby, not a horse, not a red horse."

"Is this story also too scary to act out?"

"It *is* too scary. Too scary for Fredrick. Too scary for Christopher. Playdough is my favorite color," she adds, moving to the playdough table and changing the subject.

For Fredrick, the worrisome topic is "water." His robbers and monsters do not help him when he tries to tell his story. Something is on his mind for which there is no dramatic substitute.

"Water," he dictates on Monday and then, on Tuesday, he explains. "Once there was water. You drown yourself. You stay under water."

Wednesday, it is the same: "Water. Then you drown. Water. And then you drown."

On Thursday, I ask, "Did a bad thing happen in the lake, Fredrick?"

"No."

"In a swimming pool?"

"Yeah, I drowned."

"Who pulled you out?"

"My sister took me out. In South Beach. In a pool. I went under again. And I went under again. Then my sister took me out."

I ask Fredrick's mother about the "drowning" incident. "He never even came close to drowning," she says. "His head was under for a fraction of a second. We were right there, all of us."

"But he must have been scared," I say.

"Yes, but we didn't realize it until we read the stories."

Mollie talks about the event early the next morning and then again at snacktime. "Fredrick falls off the bench in the ater. But I don't because I hold Daddy's hand once upon a time."

"Is this a story for me to write down?"

"No, it's a water thing."

"I have a water thing, too," William says. "My mother went in the sand then she found me in the water."

"Did you drowned?" Mollie asks.

"Yes."

A week later, after Erik tells him he can be the Incredible Hulk, Fredrick suddenly is able to resolve the water stories. He will become a marvelous creature who swims fast and can never be drowned. He tells his new story with breathless excitement.

"The Incredible Hulk jumps into some water and he gets his head wet. The lion tries to get me out of the water. I'm the Hulk. And I run and jump sideways into the swimming pool. And the lion tries to kill me on my head. I can swim fast, fast to the other place. And then I'm home."

Now, during playtime, Fredrick hulks around the room acting the monster. Other superheroes and monsters have also been disturbing the peace lately, but Fredrick's exuberance brings me running faster.

7

"Aren't monsters not allowed, Mrs. Paley?" Maria shouts tearfully from the doll corner. The urgency of her appeal is confirmed by the appearance of a hunched-over, grunting Fredrick pretending to devour a doll. By habit, I move to stop the intruder, then hesitate, remembering how often the children have supported his descriptions of child-eating monsters.

"I'm the Hulk," Fredrick says proudly.

"Is he a good guy or a bad guy?" I ask.

"Good guy," Adam informs us from the telephone table.
"Does he scare people who are cooking supper?"
"Just bad guys."
"Okay, Fredrick. See if there are any bad guys in here. Who are you, Adam?"
"The telephone man. I'm fixing the telephone."
Seeing no bad guys in the doll corner, Fredrick turns his attention to the cash register. Have I tricked him? I think, rather, that the children and I are learning to ask questions about the crucial issues in a preschool classroom. We are not concerned about how the color green is made. But we do need to find the logic by which private fantasies are turned into social play, and social play into a rule-governed society of children and teachers.

These matters are endlessly debatable, particularly when four- and five-year-olds sit in judgment, and the process of determining how the play goes is often more important than the play itself.

Fredrick's first social response may be to disrupt, but he is learning that the kind of play he likes best is found in dramatic scenes. Contentment lies in uncovering – not dismantling – the plot. It is clear to me that when I comment less on disruption and spend more time helping children talk about the characters and plot, the quality of the play advances. Robbers and monsters are noisy and sometimes scary, but the plot is compelling enough to stir Mollie into storytelling.

"The bad guy and the red horse."
"Is that the whole story, Mollie?"
"And a girl."
"Does she have a name?"
"No name of girl. No name. The ghost is there. There *is* a girl. A ghost and a girl."
"Does the girl do something?"
"She makes pies something and the ghost gets her pies. Then the ghost takes it away to the gorilla's house and he was very sad. And he never saw the pies again. Don't tell anyone."

Five minutes later, Mollie returns to the story table. "I'm the ghost."

"Are we going to act out your story?"

She nods. "And Fredrick is the gorilla."

Upstairs, I announce, "Mollie has decided to act out today's story. The others, she said, were too scary."

"Is this one scary?" Fredrick is always first to ask the question.

Mollie gives a "scary" look. "Everyone will get scared today," she warns.

I begin Mollie's story. "The bad guy and the red horse, and a girl. No name of girl. No name. The ghost is there. There *is* a girl. A ghost and a girl. She makes pies something and the ghost gets her pies . . . "

"Gimme back those pies!" Libby shouts. "Say that, Mollie." The children's stories are part of the unfolding culture of the group and, as in play, members of the audience feel they have the right to influence the outcome.

"Say it, Mollie," Libby persists.

Mollie imitates the older girl, then adds a new line of her own. "Gimme those pies! And the ghost gobbles it up too fast!" She stuffs her fingers into her mouth and slurps noisily. "Everybody watch me do this. It's not too scary for you now."

The whole class *is* watching Mollie. They enter her fantasy, and she is no longer an outsider. She can begin to take responsibility for the events that shape her new society, an institution that seems to organize itself around the imperative of story.

8

"Christopher is a baby," Mollie tells me. "You know what he does? He falls on Erik and he won't get up. I'm a big girl. I don't do that, right?"

"You don't do that. But, you know, Christopher *is* already three. He had his birthday in school."

"No, he's not, because I'm already three already four and I told my mother he's a baby just like Leslie."

Mollie calls Christopher a baby and Erik says he's a troublemaker, labels they do not attach to Fredrick, whose style is more familiar and more sensible.

For me, all the threes make more sense than does Christopher, who says, "Hello birthday," to me every morning. His greeting is somehow connected to the occurrence of six birthdays in September, of which one was his. Nonetheless, "Hello birthday" is jarring in its inappropriateness, especially when combined with other unexpected behaviors.

I keep trying to find ordinary explanations for Christopher's puzzling actions. After all, if Mollie calls a variety of materials her "favorite color," perhaps "Hello birthday" means "Is today someone's birthday?" or "Remember when it was my birthday?" Mollie keeps saying that tomorrow is her birthday and Libby warns children they won't be invited to hers.

Christopher also says, "I'm the elephant," the moment someone begins a story. The storyteller replies, "I'm not talking about elephants," but Christopher persists until stopped by a teacher.

Nor is it only a matter of words. He stumbles and tumbles into children's play, repeating unwanted behaviors, oblivious to consequences. They complain, threaten, and push him away; teachers are increasingly annoyed and impatient, but he continues to roll on, as if in a driverless machine.

Christopher's encroachments seem a world apart from Mollie's movable chairs. She stops spreading out the moment another child arrives, whereas Christopher seems not to notice who is present. An even more significant difference exists between Christopher and Fredrick, who also plows into other people's sand tunnels, but with full awareness.

"I was here first!" he declares. "You took too much! That's a stupid hole." He knows he must give reasons. Christopher digs into the middle of a castle as if it – and the owner – are not there.

Is something wrong with Christopher? The question is as unavoidable as it is nonproductive. The moment I decide his condition has a name, my vision becomes blurred and whatever he does or says will be prejudged. "This is the way children with this problem behave," I am bound to think. But of Mollie I say, "This is the way three-year-olds act."

9

"Good morning, Christopher."

"Hello birthday."

"Please don't say that to me any more, Christopher. Just say 'Hello' to me, okay? Not 'Hello birthday.'" Christopher looks curiously at me.

"Guess what, teacher," Mollie says. "My birthday is coming today."

"You mean tomorrow. It's coming tomorrow."

"No, it's coming today."

"Tomorrow is your real birthday, Mollie."

"Today is my coming birthday."

"Oh, I see. Your birthday is coming. It will be here tomorrow." Mollie always receives the benefit of any doubt from me.

The next morning I wait for Christopher at the door. "Hello, Christopher. Remember what I asked you to say to me?"

"Hi."

"Hi, Christopher. Good morning."

"It's my birthday."

"No, it isn't your birthday. Guess whose it is?"

"Christopher."

"Not yours, Christopher. It's Mollie's birthday. She's three years old."

"Now" and "tomorrow" and "already" and "coming" have finally merged for Mollie and prove to be more excitement than she can handle. By the time she and her mother arrive with a large box of freshly baked cupcakes, the room is filled with noisy activity, and Mollie becomes frightened. She is accustomed to beginning her school day in an empty classroom and is startled by the crowd.

"I don't want to come, Mommy. I want to go home now, Mommy."

"We can't go now, Mollie. It's your birthday. We have lovely cupcakes."

"It's coming tomorrow."

"We'll have fun, Mollie. What should we do first?" Mrs. Nardick asks, but Mollie shakes her head and climbs on her mother's lap. "Let's paint a picture, Mollie, shall we?"

"We can't paint today," Mollie says sadly.

"Can we color?"

"No, not color."

"Can I read you a book?"

"Yes." Mollie allows her mother to read, but no one may sit next to them in the library corner or, later, in the music room. Mrs. Nardick is tolerant but surprised.

"Don't worry," I whisper. "She's always friendly in class."

Christopher stares at Mollie on her mother's lap, then begins to stroke her arm. "Are you a birthday?" he asks.

"Today *is* Mollie's birthday," Mrs. Nardick replies.

"Mollie is a birthday. Me too. I'm a birthday."

"You mean, Mollie is a birthday girl? Yes, she is. Could we play with this boy, Mollie? At the playdough table?"

"He's Christopher," Mollie says, jumping down. "He's a elephant. We can make a birthday cake for Daddy."

"What do you mean, 'He's an elephant'?"

Ignoring her mother's question, Mollie begins rolling out the playdough. "I'm making cakes with dinosaurs so they

21

could eat things. Things that you make cakes for dinosaurs that you want."

"What kind of cakes do dinosaurs eat?" her mother asks.

"Chocolate birthday cake. They'll be old candles and I'll blow on them."

"How old are the dinosaurs?"

"October ninth."

"That's *your* birthday, Mollie."

"Because Daddy's birthday is number five and Leslie's is number one and Billy's going to be his birthday but he had his birthday."

"Mollie-dolly," Mrs. Nardick murmurs, reaching over to hug her daughter. "Mollie-dolly. Today is *your* birthday. Not Daddy, not Leslie, not Billy. Only my angel girl. Only Mollie."

"Okay, Mommy."

10

Christopher pushes Barney down in the playground and then again in the hallway. I stand between the boys, glaring down at Christopher.

"No, Christopher. You can't push people."

"I'm pushing Barney," he says without emotion.

"No, you must not do it. We won't let you."

"I'm pushing Barney."

"He saw someone doing it on the playground," Mrs. Alter explains. "Some boy in the other class. Now he keeps saying that he's pushing Barney."

Mollie screws up her face. "Don't push Barney!"

"Don't say it," Christopher tells her.

"Mollie can say it, Christopher. Everyone can tell you not to push Barney."

"No. Only the teacher says it."

22

He slumps against me, and my arms automatically encircle him. He needs me, I tell myself. I cannot be angry with this child.

"I like you so much, Christopher. But you must not push Barney. You'll hurt him if you do that."

Mollie runs up and throws her arms around my neck, almost toppling me. Soon, half a dozen children are hugging me. There is a sudden initimacy that includes us all.

"I like you, Mrs. Paley," Fredrick says. Christopher, still holding on to me, peers at Fredrick in surprise.

The scene does not puzzle me as it does Christopher. The children like me most when I am forgiving misdeeds, theirs or someone else's. They want me to acknowledge errant behavior without too much fuss and accept the wrongdoer into my arms. Not too strangely, I like myself best in the same role. Christopher is destined to provide me with many opportunities to demonstrate this fact.

"I've got a good idea, Christopher," I say, wanting to change the subject. "How about telling your elephant story? It will be your first story."

The children have learned to dismiss his "I'm the elephant" interruptions with a shrug and continue their stories. To me, such indifference is worse than anger. It says that they expect him to speak nonsense.

"Come on, Christopher. Sit down and tell me your elephant story so I can write it for you. You've been talking about that elephant for a long time. I'd like to know what he does when he's in a story."

Christopher takes a sheet of paper and begins to draw. "It's a elephant story," he says, handing me the hasty sketch.

"My lord, Christopher! You've drawn a real elephant!"

Mollie glances over his shoulder. "That's Baby Elephant," she announces without surprise. Her recognition stirs my memory. He has reproduced the cover of a book we read during the first week of school. Baby Elephant is lost, and before he finds his mother a number of animals offer him a home. Is this what Christopher wants from the story-

ner? Can I live with you in your story, can I be your friend, will you care for me? Or, is it *my* attention and affection he seeks?

Upstairs, Christopher swings his trunk and galumps around the room while I hold up his picture. No one asks, "Where are the words?" The children's concept of "story" includes every sort of behavior and unspoken thought.

After snack, Christopher plays Concentration with Mollie and displays almost total recall of the sixteen overturned cards. The contrast between what he can and cannot do is too great for me to put the pieces together and see the whole child. He draws a better elephant and plays a better memory game than any other child in the class, but continually misjudges his position with real children and events. Nor does he understand as well as Mollie that his visions are not necessarily seen by others.

Mollie can make the leap to my thinking in ways that Christopher resists. She told me once, "Buddy took me to the circus," giving no identity to Buddy. She assumed, as would any young child, that people she knows are also known by her teacher.

"Who is Buddy?" I asked.

"Buddy lives with Sheila."

"Who is Sheila?"

"She lives upstairs."

The next time Mollie mentions Buddy, she is more careful. "Did you see Buddy upstairs when I was at home?" She still believes that I am aware of her life outside of school, but knows she must provide a reference point if we are to have a conversation.

Christopher, on the other hand, is oblivious to another person's confusion. He tells us at snack time:

"Arlene gives me peanut butter, too."

"Is Arlene the babysitter?"

"She's a giraffe."

"Arlene gave you a toy giraffe?"

"No."

"She read a book about a giraffe?"

24

"That's Daddy's zoo book."

He labels the book but not the person who reads it to him. He combines two images, Arlene and giraffe, and gives no thought to whether the result is understood by his listeners. Yet I too presume prior knowledge on the children's part. I expect Mollie to know that purple is never called green and Christopher to realize that Arlene's primary identity is "babysitter." Mollie is more likely to call purple *green* when she wants me to stop questioning her, but why does Christopher call Arlene a giraffe? Perhaps, in a world that generally does not make sense, it seems not to matter which words are put together.

In the morning, a tumult on the stairs brings us running. Christopher has pushed Barney off the bottom step and is staring at his victim who is unhurt but crying angrily.

"Christopher! Why are you doing this? We told you not to push Barney!" Again, he collapses against me. "I'm worried about you, Christopher."

"Why are you?" His question surprises me. I am always startled when Christopher asks a direct question about an actual event.

"Because you might push Barney again. I don't want him to get hurt."

"Do you want me to get hurt?" Christopher asks.

"No, I don't want you to get hurt either."

Mollie sits next to us on the bottom step. "Do you want *me* to get hurt?" she asks.

"Not you either, Mollie."

"Do you want Fredrick to get hurt?"

"No, not Fredrick either. I don't want anyone in the class to get hurt." I turn my full attention to Christopher, smoothing his tousled hair. "Christopher, you'll have to stay next to me all morning. You can sit in my lap or in a chair or hold my hand."

"Why?"

"So I can be sure you won't push Barney. You have that idea in your mind and it keeps coming out."

"Why does Christopher have to sit on your lap?" Barney asks.

"Because he has a hard time remembering."

"Do I?"

"Not as much as Christopher. Remember when he kept saying 'Hello birthday' and I told him not to and finally he stopped?" Barney nods. "Well, now we're reminding him not to push you."

Christopher does not object to staying at my side; when he asks if he can build a spaceship, I place my chair alongside and take down stories in the blocks area. Christopher turns an imaginary steering wheel and speaks softly in two different voices.

"Why are you doing the stories in here?" Mollie asks.

"To make sure Christopher remembers not to push Barney."

"I'm making sure, too," she says, bringing a chair next to mine.

The next morning Christopher tells me he won't push Barney.

"You're sure you don't need to sit with me today?"

"I don't push Barney."

"Okay. I believe you. Do you want to play a game with me?"

Mollie trails after us. "Will you push Barney?"

"No."

"Now you can have blackberries and milk." She quotes from "Peter Rabbit" whose well-behaved siblings are given blackberries and milk while naughty Peter drinks camomile tea.

"Because I didn't eat Mr. McGregor's lettuce?"

"Right. Now you're a good boy."

The issue of crime and punishment is viewed best in Mr. McGregor's garden, especially as Mollie is guilty of similar misdeeds at home and, in fact, decides to push Christopher off his chair at snack time.

"Why did you do that, Mollie?"

"Because he pushed Barney."

"He isn't going to do that any more, and you mustn't either."

"Daddy spanks me to push Leslie."

"Then don't push Leslie either."

"I don't push Leslie either or else."

"Is Leslie your baby, Mollie?" Christopher asks. "Are you her brother?"

"I'm a sister. She's not a boy brother."

"Hey, Mollie. *I'm* a boy brother!"

"You can't be a sister, right, Christopher?"

"Yeah. Christopher is my brother."

"No," Mollie corrects him. "*You* are Christopher's brother."

Christopher gives Mollie a big grin. He is having a real conversation, perhaps his first one at school.

"This is school," Mollie says. "This is my school."

"This is school," Christopher repeats.

11

Several children regularly arrive early now. Mollie is still first, but Maria follows in five or ten minutes.

"I hear Maria," Mollie says. "What are those things?"

"What things?"

"The step things."

"Oh, you mean the footsteps."

Mollie shakes her head. "They're called *step*-foots. They come from the steps. You have to say *step*-foots."

Maria smiles when she sees Mollie. "Hello, Mollie. You were first."

"Look at my flower shirt, Maria. Do you want to help zip in your coat? Do you want to help?"

"What?"

"Do you want to help zip in your nice blue sweater?"

"It's a jogging coat," Maria tells her.

27

"It's a jogging coat. Oh, a jogging coat. You got to help your mommy if you want to get that off."

Maria examines Mollie closely. "You mean my mommy has to help *me*."

"My mommy has to help *me*."

"Teacher, am I first on the story list?" Maria asks.

"So far you're the only one on the list."

"I'm first," Mollie says.

"You can't be first if I'm first, Mollie. You have to be called next."

"Okay then, Maria. I'm next-first." She copies Maria's actions closely, picking the same color crayons and paper. Mollie is pleased to have a big girl all to herself for this brief period every morning. Had Maria told her to say "footsteps" she would not have said "step-foots." When Maria questioned Mollie's overuse of red paint, she abandoned red for a week.

"I'm going to make a bell out of this blue paper," Maria tells us.

"Will it be loud enough if it's made of paper?" I ask.

"I can cut my bell loud enough. I can make it loud or real soft. Can I have a piece of string?"

"Sure. Can I help you with anything, Maria?"

"You could cut out my bell."

I cut the outline she has drawn and hold the string while she tapes it to the paper.

"Mrs. Paley, this is not loud enough. We have to do like this." She taps her finger against the bell.

"Maria, it does look like a bell but it doesn't sound like a bell."

"That's because I didn't make it loud enough."

"How could you make it loud enough?"

"It's almost loud enough already."

"I've got a bell at home, Maria," Mollie says.

"Is it made of paper?" I ask.

"It's made of white "

"Of something white. Is it hard or is it soft?"

"It's a circle bell."

"Maria is trying to figure out how this bell can be made louder," I say to Erik, who has just walked in.

"I'll *tell* everyone the bell is ringing," Maria decides. "I'll say 'ring-ring.' "

"Can I ring your bell?" Mollie asks.

"That ain't no bell!" Erik states. "Maria, you got to put inside some jingling batteries."

Maria has begun to color her bell blue. "My bell is the soft kind for when people are sleeping," she says.

"Oh, that kind."

"I'll make you a bell, Erik. Do you want me to?"

"Never mind."

Mollie is particularly curious about the attention Maria gives to Erik. "Is Erik in your story, Maria?"

"Erik is Spiderman," Maria replies. "But I don't know if he will be."

"Are you my *friend?*" Mollie asks, sounding as if the question is, "Are you what is called a friend?" Maria nods.

There are six names on the list by the time Maria tells her story. "Once upon a time Wonderwoman went to sleep and then a wicked old witch came and knocked her out but not really. You can be the witch, Mollie."

"I want to be a ghost."

Barely skipping a beat, Maria continues. "And then the ghost comes and picks me up." Spotting Erik in the cubby room, she calls out, "Do you want to be Spiderman, Erik?"

"No. Only if John is Batman."

"Okay. Then Spiderman and Batman came and put a rope on the ghost."

"Then I don't want to be the ghost then," Mollie says quickly.

"Yes, you can be, Mollie, because the ghost can't be tied up because you can't tie up a ghost. Then we go home and then we eat supper and then we go to sleep."

Not every storyteller is as accommodating as Maria, but most children will go a long way to include Erik and John, whose intense friendship is watched over by everyone. Some quality of their relationship suggests mysterious and exciting possibilities, especially to children who are just beginning to ask one another, "Are you my friend?"

To this question, the threes respond "yes" or "no" indiscriminately. "I'm not your friend" brings instant tears, but moments later the tearful child says to someone else, "I'm not *your* friend."

The difference between games and the real thing is sensed, but, just as Mollie does not yet imagine that red can't be substituted for yellow if one is to produce green, the necessary conditions for serious friendship are difficult to grasp.

My perspective of John and Erik differs from the one commonly held by their classmates. That which I call possessiveness, the children see as an enviable closeness; what to me is an excess of bragging and insensitivity strikes them as novel and adventurous.

Erik runs in and shouts, "Squeaky! Me and John came at the same time. I knocked your brains out, John."

"Can't do. My brains are steel. If my brains touch you, you break into atoms."

"Hello, Erik," Maria says softly.

"Who cares!" he replies.

"So what!" adds John.

The noise level rises the moment the two boys join forces, but tensions that are upsetting to me are often welcomed by those who would gladly exchange calmness for dramatic conflict.

"Don't just barge in, boys," I say. "This was a very nice spaceship until you messed it up."

"They *want* us to blow it up."

"It's Star Wars," Barney agrees blissfully.

Fredrick actually becomes more reasonable as he searches for ways to enter Erik's play. "Can I be Darth?" he pleads. "I wasn't Darth for a long time."

"You aren't playing, Fredrick."

"Can I be a robot?"

"Yeah, go on, be a robot. Do it over there."

Hurriedly, Franklin persuades Mrs. Alter to make him an

R2D2 chest cover, marked with knobs and wires, and a square mask.

"Look, Erik. I'm R2D2. Can I play? Make me a light saber, okay?"

Erik examines the robot outfit. "Okay, sit by that steering wheel. Don't shoot till I tell you."

Mollie never asks Erik and John to play, but she makes them the monsters in her stories. Their behavior at Mollie's birthday party seemed monstrous enough to her mother.

"They kept saying the cupcakes were disgusting," Mrs. Nardick tells me a few days later, "and if you touched them you would die. Then Erik stuffed the whole cupcake into his mouth and pretended to gag."

"Heavens! That does sound awful."

"Worst of all, when I criticized them on the way home, Mollie said, 'They're my friends.' That's the first time she called anyone at school a friend."

"The children like Erik and John. They find most of what the boys do authentic and fascinating."

"Authentic what?"

"Maybe authentic big-boy-best-friend stuff. Whatever it is, the children perceive it differently than we do."

Certainly Erik's bravado does not offend Mollie, and she is curious to know what it means. Maria is her resource person.

"Is Erik your friend, Maria?"

"Yes. Sometimes. He likes John more."

"Why?"

"Because John likes him."

"Because John is Robin?" Mollie wonders.

"Maybe. Maybe because John is Battle Cat."

"Is Libby your friend?"

"Yeah."

"Because she's not Robin? Because she's Wonderwoman?"

"Sometimes."

Mollie ponders these possibilities while she and Maria cut paper and make envelopes. Mollie and I no longer play "eggs in the nest" when she arrives. She has transferred her attention to Maria, who makes envelopes and friends with enviable ease. In less than two months of school Mollie has discovered that the things she most wants to learn will be revealed by other children, not by me. In particular, she wishes to find out how children grow in connectedness and sees it has much to do with the fantasy roles they play.

12

Learning is a reciprocal process; Mollie is as much teacher as student. She tells Christopher that he, like Peter Rabbit, will have blackberries and milk if he is good, and warns Margaret not to dial the fire department because Curious George "false alarmed them." She urges Erik to plant the seeds he finds in the playground so he can climb up the beanstalk "when the giant is not there," and asks Emily to help her build a brick house "so the wolf doesn't huff us."

Mollie at three displays a natural affinity for life as art. Such is the instinct of all children, of course, but in Mollie the impulse finds clear expression in words. She knows how to bring book characters into conversation, play, and stories, and the new stories she creates out of old ones produce an exciting sense of continuity.

Today, for example, she puts "Mushroom in the Rain," "The Three Pigs," and "Hansel and Gretel" into a Wonderwoman story. In the original "Mushroom in the Rain," a butterfly, a mouse, and a sparrow are drenched in a heavy downpour, then sheltered under a mushroom by a kindly ant. A frightened rabbit and a hungry fox also enter the story, but Mollie gives star billing to the wet butterfly.

"I want to be the wet butterfly and Wonderwoman. First he goes under the mushroom. Now we got to do the big, bad wolf and the three pigs and the fox is going to catch the butterfly and put it in the cage, that one from Hansel. Then Wonderwoman comes. Then I open the cage and the wet butterfly goes under the mushroom because the ant says to come in."

How has Mollie learned to integrate these bits and pieces into a sensible whole? No one else offers Christopher blackberries and milk if he is good, or unites the big, bad wolf with a fox to make trouble for a butterfly. However, it is the sort of storytelling that is heard every day during play: Cinderella and Darth Vader put the baby to bed while Superman serves tea and saves the baby from the witch just as Daddy comes home from work and sits down to eat a birthday cake.

If Mollie is quicker than most to transfer the process into her stories it is because, more than most children, she sees life as a unified whole. To her, fantasy characters and real people all communicate in the same language. It is a lesson Christopher must learn, and Mollie is becoming his primary teacher.

"Christopher, you can be the baby elephant in my story," she offers. "Because you want to, right?"

"I'm a eli-lion," he says.

"Eli-*phant*. Say 'ele-*phant*.'"

"Eli-lion."

"What is an eli-lion?" I ask.

"A meli-lion."

I persist with my questions. "Does it have a trunk? Does it roar?"

"Teli-lion."

Mollie knows how to bring Christopher back to her. "There *is* a eli-lion in my story, Christopher. And a ghost. And then they get scared and fall down."

Christopher smiles. "*I* get scared and fall down, right? And then I roar up to the sky."

"And a piece of sky falls on us it's Chicken Licken," Mollie continues.

"And we go to tell the king?"

"Yes. That's in my story, too."

She does a better job than I can of putting Christopher's ideas into a recognizable context, because she and Christopher think alike. Mollie would not have told Christopher to stop saying "Hello birthday"; she would have called *him* Hello Birthday. "Do you want to be Hello Birthday in my story, Christopher? You be Hello Birthday and I'll be Strawberry Shortcake."

She accepts his differences as style, not deficiency, and plays along with confusing behavior until it becomes more familiar. Enigmas are unraveled by pretending they are something else.

Mollie is sometimes better at explaining Christopher's meaning than her own.

"Mrs. Alter is sick today," I tell Mollie. "Another teacher is coming. Miss Barton."

"What does Miss Barton mean?"

"That's her name. Miss Barton is the teacher who is coming."

"Where does that come from?"

"Where does *she* come from?"

"Where does *that* come from?"

"If you mean Miss Barton, she's called a substitute teacher. She helps out when teachers are sick."

"Why *is* she Miss Barton?"

"That's her name, Mollie, just as mine is Mrs. Paley."

"Why *does* she Miss Barton?"

Her question remains a mystery. Does Mollie herself know the question? Is it the "Miss" part that sounds odd since the other teachers are called "Mrs."? Perhaps "Barton" reminds her of another word, and she cannot explain the connection. With three-year-olds one must expect a number of misunderstandings, no matter how conscientiously a point is pursued. Yet the children always seem to understand one another.

13

"Are you a sister, Margaret?"

"I'm a brother's sister."

Mollie and Margaret cut and fold paper at the six-foot round table we call the story table which is also the repository for crayons, scissors, paste, and paper.

"They call a brother they sometimes call a boy," Mollie states.

"Brothers are boys, girls are girls."

"You're a girl, Margaret."

"So are you, Mollie, L-M-N-O. That spells 'girl.' "

"You don't know how to make a triangle," Mollie retorts. Her swift mood change seems related to Margaret's apparent ability to spell. One three-year-old never knows the probable limits of another's powers unless, of course, they are pretending to be other characters. Little girls pretending to be little girls in the doll corner know exactly what little girls can and cannot do.

"Yes, I do! Teacher, Mollie says I can't make triangles!"

"Show her, Margaret."

"I *do* know how. And I can make a hexigon and you're not my friend, Mollie."

"Yes, you *can* make a triangle, Margaret," Mollie says. "You really can. Let's play in the doll corner. Let's be kittens, okay?"

"Yeah, let's be real kittens."

"Are you a hexigon kitty?" Mollie asks, setting the table.

"I'm the mother."

"We're both mothers. Leslie is the baby."

Mollie doesn't know that real babies, the ones at home, are not mentioned in the doll corner. The whole point of pretending to be a baby is to review the subject one step removed, in the abstract.

"I'll be the baby," Margaret says, curling up in the crib. "Tell me to go to bed. Are you angry?"

35

"Go to bed! I'm angry!" Mollie shouts.

"Then you have to go to bed too, Mommy, so I won't cry."

"Oh, oh, nighttime. Go to bed!"

"Oh, oh, morning. Wake up."

"Oh, oh, nighttime. Go to bed."

"Oh, oh, morning. Wake up."

The girls repeat their game six more times before they are ready to change the plot. This is typical of their doll corner dialogue if there are no older children around.

"Oh, oh, I'm the daddy," Margaret decides. "I'm going to work."

"I'm the mommy. Hot porridge. I'm the middle-sized bear. Someone's been eating my porridge and they ate the baby's porridge all up."

The girls return to the story table and push two chairs together. "Look, teacher. I'm sitting next to Mollie because we're both sisters."

Mollie blushes with the pleasure of new intimacy. "You can *too* make a triangle, Margaret. You're a big girl. Teacher, I told Margaret that she's a big girl."

The girls smile at each other. For twenty minutes they have practiced friendship and controversy in comfortable doses, but now Maria, Samantha, and Erik run in laughing and all attention centers on them.

"Hey, did you see the Dukes last night? You shoulda seen that! It was so funny. Here's what Bo did. B-r-r! Ow! Yikes! Watch out! I'm crashing!" Erik races around the table, then falls on the floor, his legs straight up. The girls laugh appreciatively.

Later, Mollie returns to the doll corner and watches Libby and Maria act out a far more complicated bedtime scene than the one she and Margaret played.

"Mommy! Mommy! Spank this child! My sister's not being nice to me."

"I'll put you in your bed and you'll be sorry."

"She's out! She's out!"

"Now you! Stop that! She's trying to go to sleep, sister."

"She's crying. My brother is too noisy. Spank him."

"No, go to bed! And stay there!"

"Get that little girl and put her in jail. She's waking up the baby."

Erik, John, and Adam burst in. "You're under arrest. We're the police. Where's that bad girl you said?"

"Get out! No boys in this house!"

"We don't have to get out, dum-dum."

"Here's the tea. Sit over there. Tea-time, father. It's tea-time."

"We're the bad guys. We killed the other monster. We broke the crib."

Mollie rocks her doll in the crib, trying to put its arm in a dress sleeve. "Erik," she says, "can you put the baby's dress on?"

"Huh? Uh, okay. I can do it." He stops pretending to axe the crib, picks up the doll and carefully slips on and buttons its dress. "I know how to button anything," he tells the group.

14

"I'm a honker with a purple thing," Mollie says on Halloween morning. "Make me a honker."

Mrs. Alter and I are fashioning costumes from tissue, crepe paper, and yarn.

"What *is* a honker, Mollie?"

"That's what you do with your thing."

"You honk?"

"On Halloween you honk. It's a nose. A yellow nose. You go 'honk, honk.'"

"Guess what?" Erik asks. "I'm Skeletor. He has to have blue bones. John is He-Man and guess what? I'm going to jump up and knock him out and guess what's going to happen? He's going to jump away and I'm going to go tumbling around the room. I need a sword. Also, John needs a sword."

"Do I need a sword, Erik? I'm a honker."

"No, you don't."

"Erik, do you know what a honker is?" I ask.

"No. It's something it doesn't have a sword."

"I'm telling a Halloween story," says Mollie. "About a snake and a Peter and the Wolf and a banana."

"Is that a Halloween story?"

"About the banana and Peter and the Wolf and a pumpkin and . . ." Mollie is stumped. She cannot imagine the attributes of a Halloween story. However, later, as she listens to Samantha's story the focus becomes clear.

"We were painting the pumpkins in the woods," Samantha says, "and the witch comes. Then the witch took off her mask. It was Amelia."

"Wait! I didn't finish my Halloween story," Mollie exclaims. "So the wolf came and got the pumpkin."

"Are you the wolf, Mollie?"

"I'm the pumpkin that gets the wolf. Wait, it's not finished yet. *Then* the pumpkin came and got the wolf. You have to say *'then'*!"

In rapid succession, Mollie solves several problems. She satisfies the needs of a Halloween story by having a wolf steal the pumpkin; she rearranges the facts to enable the pumpkin to get the wolf, since she is to be the pumpkin; finally, she puts the story into proper narrative form by using the word "then."

Mollie sees no need to count eggs and brushes the same way every day or stick to a consistent time sequence for her birthday, but she can handle complex issues when they are part of a story, whether in prose or in play. If she can *pretend* something is happening, the rules that govern the event are then easier to view.

Christopher, on the other hand, counts correctly every time and remembers that blue mixed with yellow turns to green. But he finds it hard to alter a pattern of thought once it has formed. He has been listening to children announce their costume choices, and when I ask for his decision he tells a story instead. Since we are at the story table we must be telling stories.

"Have you decided what costume you want, Christopher?"

"The tiger rides on Mr. Penny."

"A tiger costume? Black and yellow stripes?"

"Mr. Penny rides on the tiger."

"Do you want to be Mr. Penny? I can make a zoo keeper badge. Okay? We're making costumes now."

"And then the tiger rides the man."

"I'll make you some tiger ears."

"No."

"Mollie, could you help us, please?" I ask. "I'm not sure what kind of costume Christopher wants."

"Do you want to be a honker? You could be a honker, okay?"

"No."

"He is telling a story about Mr. Penny and the tiger," I tell Mollie.

"Then you could be Mr. Penny because the honker lives with the tiger in the zoo and then you can feed me fish because that's what honkers eat."

"*I'm* the tiger, Mollie, and you be the honker," Christopher says slowly, as if inventing the idea, "and we *both* eat fish."

"Then shall I make you some black and yellow stripes?" I ask.

"And yellow and black ears," he adds.

As soon as I decide that Christopher's inflexibility is *too* exceptional, some ordinary classroom event puts his behavior in better perspective for me. At cleanup time, Mollie, Barney, and Carrie show a mind-set similar to Christopher's when they scrub a clean table simply because it usually serves as the playdough table.

"But this table is already clean," I point out. "Look at the little table. We used that one for playdough today. Remember?"

"Why did the dirty part go there?" Barney asks.

"We needed the playdough table for the costumes. For all the yarn and colored paper."

"How did it get clean?" Mollie stares at the playdough table, puzzled.

"We never made it dirty, Mollie. I put the playdough over there today."

"Oh. The dirty part got over there at the other cleanup time." Satisfied with Mollie's answer, the children proceed to clean the imposter table.

15

The fours would probably not have washed a clean table or, having begun, would see their error and laugh at themselves. They are moving away from the little rituals of the threes, who can make permanent games of almost any behavior that is repeated more than once.

Stuart and Emily, for example, have a game they call "Woof-woof." The rules are as simple as the morning-nighttime game Mollie and Margaret play in the doll corner. Emily takes the blue stuffed dog, Stuart the orange one, and they carry the animals into every room saying, "Woof-woof." The fours watch them but do not participate. When Emily gives Amelia the orange dog and says, "Woof-woof," Amelia responds, kindly, "I'm four and a half."

Mollie plays an equally uncomplicated game with Barney on an L-shaped block structure. Mollie cuts a strip of paper, saying, "Here, take a piece," after which Barney takes the paper and Mollie shouts, "Good! You did it!" Now the order is reversed, with Barney cutting and Mollie taking.

"Why not do your cutting on the table?" I suggest, surveying the messy floor.

"We can't," Mollie replies. "You have to be on this kind of blocks." Since the game began on a certain block arrangement, it is a necessary part of the procedure. The fours would evolve a more complicated scheme, but the threes continue the original rules and call it "Mollie's game." When the older children interrupt these gentle pastimes, I worry about the incongruous tone of the more mature players.

Mollie, Stuart, and Margaret are absorbed in their latest version of "Are you my friend?" in which one child answers no, then repeats the question to the next person.

"Are you my friend, Stuart?"

"No. Are you my friend, Mollie?"

"No. Are you my friend, Margaret? Now say yes. Now we all have to say yes, okay?"

Libby rushes into the doll corner, breathless. "Watch out, Mollie. Move! Samantha, hurry! Scream when you see John!"

"Can I do it?" Mollie asks.

"Hide, Amelia. Under there. Boys can't come in. No boys in here."

"No you don't, Libby," John shouts. "I'm Tri-Klops. Dump it out. I broke my leg."

"Well, I'm Trap Jaw," Erik says. "I'm eating this chair. Get off, Stuart."

"No you don't," Libby warns. "No chair-eating in houses."

"Only girls live in houses," Maria calls from the crib. "Except if they're fathers."

"I'm a girl," Margaret says happily.

"I'm a girl," Mollie echoes.

Erik sticks out his tongue. "I'm a girl. I'm a pearl. I'm a yucky-fucky."

"O-o-o! I'm telling!" Samantha and Libby yell together.

"Are you a girl, Erik?" Mollie asks.

"No he ain't a girl, *girl!*" Maria screams. "Can't you see he ain't a girl? Are you crazy?"

"Don't touch that, Adam," Libby demands. "That's no business of yours. Adam, you want to be the father?"

"No business of yours, Mollie," Margaret repeats.

"Well, I'm doing my own something business," Mollie answers. "You don't have some own something."

I ask myself: Has the play in the doll corner been spoiled or improved for the threes? The hypnotic chanting of "Are you my friend?" received a discordant blast from the older children, but is the disruption necessarily bad?

Mollie, in fact, seems to benefit from the more realistic, confrontational approach of the four-year-old girls. When she claims later that Margaret is not Maria's friend, Maria refuses to enter the spirit of the game.

"You're lying, Mollie! Margaret is too my friend! She came to my house once. You're a liar!"

Mollie is astonished. She has heard the girls warn each other, "You're not coming to my house," but here is a visit that actually took place.

"Margaret is coming to *my* house today," Mollie says suddenly. "She's coming to my birthday."

At dismissal time, Mollie refuses to release Margaret's hand when her friend's mother appears. Boldly, Mollie says, "Margaret has to come to my house now."

Mrs. Silver smiles. "Maybe one day soon, but she can't come today."

Mollie begins to cry. "Today. Today she has to. Because I told her today. Because she's my friend now."

"I'll call your mother tonight. You're Mollie, right?"

"My mommy is Rita," Mollie sobs.

"Are you my friend?" will never again be so innocent a game for Mollie. This particular ritualized response may now be subjected to outside confirmation. The transition is not easy but, if she wants to know what the big girls know, Mollie will have to heed their objections when she confuses her private game with verifiable events.

42

16

The note pinned to Margaret, "Please send Margaret home with Mollie today," is a symbol of adult reality; the girls must play out the new relationship in different terms.

Mollie has been sitting at the top of the stairs and jumps up the moment she sees Margaret.

"We both have tights on," Mollie begins.

"Mine are red."

"My *shirt* is red, Margaret." She follows her friend into the cubby room. "We both have blue on our coats. Do you want to sit on a rocking chair?"

"Do you want to play with the doll house furniture, Mollie?"

"My name is Strawberry Shortcake."

"My name is Lemon Meringue."

"Mine is bumpety-bump down the stairs."

"Mine is lumpety-lump down the stairs."

"You're coming to my house, Margaret."

"I know."

Erik and John are also going home together, but Erik's possessive feelings for John are the kind Mollie reserves for her mother. He objects loudly when John agrees to be the monster in Mollie's story.

"If you do you can't come to my house, John."

John returns quickly to his seat, but I call him back. "That's not fair, John. Come on, Erik, be a good sport, won't you?"

"You could be a monster, Erik," Mollie says. "There's really two monsters." She has seen Maria handle similar situations and now Mollie can display her own growing skill as a mediator.

From the children's point of view my response is illogical, for friends must not be separated. Friendship is the supreme state of being; all demonstrations of the condition are proper and desirable. Jealousy is an acceptable human frailty that hovers over every relationship and every activity.

It is especially easy to witness in the doll corner, where family matters dominate. Samantha and Amelia are there now, covered with veils and shawls, chanting, "We're getting married." Libby enters, frowning; she senses she is being left out of an important ceremony.

"What are you doing, Samantha?"

"Watch out, Libby. We're getting married."

"Can I get married with you?"

"Hurry up, Amelia. Put on the lace, honey."

"Just us, Libby."

"I'm getting married too," Libby says. "By myself."

"Not with us, Libby, 'cause you didn't see my flower girl dress and only Amelia saw it."

"I saw my own flower girl dress and *I'm* going to the ballet."

"So am I," Samantha counters.

"I'm going to *be* the ballet."

"Well, I know how to dance and you don't."

"Yes I do!" Libby begins to cry. "Teacher, Samantha says I can't dance."

"I'm sure you can, Libby."

"She's stupid! She's a liar."

Mollie has been watching the scene from the telephone table. She walks over to the two angry girls and smiles. "Guess what! Margaret's coming to my house today. She's my friend."

Her declaration is not out of context. The argument she interrupts is not about marriage or the ballet, but concerns who is playing with whom. This is the proper time to announce that she will play with Margaret, all by herself, at her house today.

The girls look at Mollie and Margaret and remember that they too are friends. Samantha dials the telephone. "Hello, Libby? Call the police. There's a noise. I think it's a lion."

"Yeah. I hear roaring. Turn off the light. Pretend we're not home."

Margaret takes Mollie's hand as they leave. Neither one is comfortable in the doll corner when the lion is at the door.

17

A few minutes later Mollie returns, uncertainly. She knows the girls are only pretending something bad is about to happen; but what if the bad thing doesn't know it's pretend? Nonetheless, Mollie decides to stay, keeping one foot outside the drama.

"Go to sleep, Mollie," Libby orders. "There might be something dangerous. You won't like it."

"I know it," Mollie says. "But I got a bunk bed at home and I sleep there."

"Bunk beds are too scary," Amelia says.

"Why are they?" Mollie looks worried.

"It's a monster, Mollie. Hide!"

"I know. But there's no monsters in my house today."

"You have to hide, Mollie. It's a real monster."

"I'm going to hide by the teacher."

"No, Mollie, stay here. Under here. Under the cover."

"I'm going to be a statue," Mollie whispers. "So he won't see me."

"He won't get me," Libby says, "because I've got a real gun. You want one?"

Mollie shakes her head. "I'm a statue."

"No, Mollie, hide. Come here. I'll hide you. The boys are going to scare us." Libby looks around for an available boy and catches sight of Fredrick at the painting table. "Watch out!" she shouts. "Fredrick is coming! He's a monster! Hide!"

Fredrick drops his brushes and rushes into the doll corner on all fours. "Roar!" He arches his back and claws the air. "G-r-r!"

"Teacher! Fredrick's scaring Mollie!"

"I'm a lion. I'm roaring."

"Is he scaring you, Mollie?"

"No."

"Is anyone scaring you?"

"The bunk bed," she answers solemnly.

I return to the story table and the play continues.

"Now it's your turn to be scared," Libby tells Samantha.

"Oh, oh. Nobody's there. Help me, help me!"

"Here's your cup," Mollie says. "I'm wearing blue tights. Look, Samantha. It's hot chocolate."

"Ding-dong. The babysitter is here. She scared away the monster. Time for your bath, Mollie."

Suddenly the girls are dressing dolls and cooking supper. The monster is gone in a flurry of simple domestic routines. Mollie has not learned to chase it away by saying, "There is no monster; it's bathtime," though she did attempt to distract it with her blue tights and hot chocolate.

Mollie is a more confident storyteller than doll-corner actor, though this was not always the case. In the beginning, the ghosts in her stories were "too scary for people." Now she creates and abolishes ghosts with aplomb, but does not feel similarly in control when monsters are conjured up by others. Their play might be the real pretend; her storytelling, she knows, is just pretend pretend.

Nonetheless, she cannot help but notice that one way the big girls deal with monsters is to identify more conspicuously as *girls* in the company of other girls, deliberately separating themselves from those most likely to act the monster: the boys.

After one particularly raucous encounter, I ask Mollie why Libby is making such a fuss with the boys.

"The big boys are nice to me," Mollie answers.

"But not to Libby?"

"Libby is the mother."

"Does the mother have to scold the boys?"

"The boys have to go outside to play."

Mollie is certainly aware that mothers are likely to resist some of the roles boys play, but later, in the climbing room, Mollie happens upon another piece of the puzzle.

The threes are upstairs for a brief period of private play. Normally the younger group includes five girls and six boys. Today, with four boys absent, the upstairs contingent consists of Mollie, Margaret, Emily, Sybil, and Carrie, along with Barney and William.

Mollie immediately notices the imbalance. "There's too many girls," she tells me.

"There *are* more girls here today," I say. "Four boys are sick."

"Catch my feet, Mollie," Margaret shouts. "Try to catch my feet. I'm on the top of the mountain."

Some of the children are with Margaret on the ladders, while others are making a school bus with the benches and crates in the music room. Barney sits alone in a large wooden box.

"This is *my* house!" he calls out.

"Can I come in?" Mollie asks.

"No."

"Me, Barney?" requests Margaret, from the ladder.

"No. Not you!"

"Just me?" William asks.

"Yeah, just you. Just William. No one else."

Mollie glances around the room and runs back to the ladder. "Well, this is *our* house and Barney and William can't come in. Barney and William are . . . boys!"

"Can I, Mollie?" Emily and Carrie call out at the same time.

"Yes, you and you and you and you can come in the girls' house," Mollie declares grandly. "This is the girls' house. *That's* the boys' house. All the girls come here."

"Yeah, this *is* the boys' house," William and Barney tell each other.

The children gaze at the two structures in a moment of silent wonder, then begin to chant, "Boys' house, girls' house!" Quite by accident, Mollie has made an important discovery. Had all six boys been present, they would not have gotten together in the same structure. With two boys in the box, Mollie glimpses the separation alluded to in the doll corner.

"Girls' house, boys' house!" Mollie gives a final shout and

jumps off the ladder. The game is over and the boys and girls mix together again on the school bus. For a few moments, a random selection of three-year-olds organized themselves into two distinct communities. The collective strength of each was noted briefly, then shelved for a later time.

18

The girls' house has no immediate influence on Mollie, who continues to interchange male and female characters in her play and stories for the rest of the school year. The concept of separation comes across in terms of age instead. With the new upstairs play period Mollie seems to realize for the first time that she is a member of a group differentiated by the number three. Labels such as "snack group" and "younger children" take on a new meaning.

"Fredrick, are you a big boy? Are you a little bit big?"

"Yeah, I'm already three."

"Hey, I'm three, too! I'm a big girl. Hello? Hello? Ring-ring. Who's there for supper?"

"Should I come now for supper?"

"Are you at the office? Come at six o'clock four o'clock. Did you cash the check?"

John comes in, followed by several older children, all wearing numbered cardboard police badges.

"Mollie, I need the phone. It's the police."

Mollie quickly moves to a corner doll bed, and John takes her place at the telephone table. "Police! Somebody's breakin' houses and golden chairs. Snatching things."

Erik picks up the other telephone. "Okay. I'll come over. Goodbye, man."

"Goodbye, man."

"Hey, somebody's stealing bicycles," Libby calls out.

"Mollie, did somebody rob you? Some robber took your bicycle!"

"No, they didn't. I'm three years old."

Christopher stands at the doorway. "I'm a police," he says. "I'm a police, Erik."

"No, you're not," John tells him. "You're not playing."

"Yes, I *am* a police," Christopher repeats, knocking over the telephone and dumping the pencils on the floor.

Erik grabs his arm. "Hey! This is our police station. Put this guy in jail."

"Yeah, lock him up," Libby agrees. "He can't knock down telephones."

"I'm the elephant. Number four elephant."

"No you're not! No elephants, Christopher!"

"Shoot the elephants," Christopher whispers.

"Police! Get this boy. Put him in jail in one hour. One minute."

"One minute for the elephant," Christopher says, struggling to loosen Erik's grip.

"Christopher, are you three years old?" Mollie's question breaks through the tumult and Erik releases Christopher, who runs to Mollie and sits beside her on the bed.

"I got three on my birthday, that other day," Christopher says.

"Me, too," Mollie states happily, taking Christopher's hand. "We're *both* the same three and so is Fredrick. He *told* me."

The police leave and Mollie is alone with Christopher. "Here's your birthday cake. It's your party." She rolls out a cylinder of playdough. "And here's your older candle. Elephants need big candles."

"I'm a boy."

"You *are* a boy."

"Yes."

"I'm a girl. *Pretend* I'm a girl, Christopher. Pretend it's my three-year-old birthday. Pretend I invited you to my three-year-old birthday."

49

Mollie and Christopher look at each other, shyly. Does something seem different? For Mollie, at least, the demarcation line between fantasy and reality has suddenly become so bright that she can imagine herself as a three-year-old girl who is about to have a birthday party.

19

Mollie can also light up the boundaries for Christopher when he drifts off course, as he does the next day in a lotto game.

"Who has the fruit basket?" Samantha asks, holding up a lotto card.

"I do!" Mollie calls out.

"Who has the bicycle?"

"Trick or treat!" Christopher replies.

Samantha is annoyed. She has no patience for Christopher when he speaks nonsense. "Stop that! It's a bicycle!"

"It's trick or treat. Trick or treat bicycle."

Mollie opens her tiny purse and gives Christopher a plastic coin. "Here's your trick or treat. Ring the bell and say 'trick or treat.' "

"Ring-ring. Trick or treat."

"Here you go." She gives him another coin. "Okay, now give it back to me."

"Now you do it to me, Mollie."

"After this game, okay? Because I'm playing this lotto game."

Christopher runs off, unwilling to accommodate to the lotto game, but indirectly acknowledging that "trick or treat" belongs to another kind of play. I am painfully conscious of the fact that my own response to Christopher would have sounded more like Samantha's than Mollie's.

Just as I keep comparing myself to Mollie in our approaches to Christopher, I also use Mollie as the standard by which to judge him. He, for example, can build a better block structure, but does not know how to get someone to play in it. In September, Mollie was also unprepared to invite another child to play – but she watched and learned. Now she is quick to initiate play and respond to its fluctuations.

"Carrie, you want to come in my candy house?"

"I'm making a boat."

"It *is* a boat. It's a candy boat," Mollie says, peering at Carrie between two wooden cylinders.

"Are you a monster, Mollie?"

Mollie looks surprised. "Yes, I am!" she squeals, running around in the block area.

"No, you're *not* a monster."

"Hide from me, Carrie. You hide from me."

"No, I'm making a boat."

"This is my monster seat."

"No monster seat, Mollie!"

"G-r-r! Look, teacher. I'm a dragon monster. Look, Carrie."

"This is my bed, Mollie. It's a beddy boat."

"Where's *my* beddy boat?"

"This is your beddy boat here, Mollie. Let's both be mothers. Bring the dolls."

"Let's be the sister. The mother-sister."

Later, Mollie resurrects her monster when Maria tells a story. "Once upon a time a little girl went to her house. There was no monster in there and . . . "

"A dragon monster came? Did that happen?"

Maria nods. "But there was a dragon monster came and she ran into the house."

"She should of beat him on the head," Erik comments from the sand table.

"Girls don't do that," Maria responds with great dignity. "*This* girl don't do that."

"Well, the girl in *my* story does it. Can I tell mine right now, teacher? I can't wait a minute!"

51

"You're not next on the list, Erik," I say.

"I have to! I can't wait!"

"Okay. Go ahead. If no one minds."

"There was this little girl and she beats a monster on the head because he wasn't looking at the way she was coming." He speaks directly to the children assembled at the table waiting to tell their stories. "So then she saw the three bears, and then the cave where they lived exploded, and then a monster came and killed the bears, and the little girl beat him on the head."

"Was it Goldilocks?" Mollie asks.

"Yeah, it *was* Goldilocks."

"I'm Goldilocks," Mollie announces as she begins her story. "And there's a baby bear. And the sister bear. Maria is the mother bear. Erik is the daddy bear. Then a wolf came in the cave and scared them away and they never came by Goldilocks again."

Mollie's eyes glow with the sense of belonging. "I told the same kind Erik did. Say it when we're upstairs, teacher. Say it's the same kind like Erik."

"I want to do that too," Stuart says. "The mama bear made porgy. Then a girl comes. Goldilocks comes. And a once upon a time part. And the wolf."

Even Carrie, who limits herself to kittens, yields to the spirit of the group. "The kitty says, 'meow.' And then the bears come."

Finally it is Christopher's turn. "It's a purple armadillo," he says. "And it rides on the tiger."

"Then do they see the three bears?" Mollie prompts. She assumes that Christopher wants to tie his story to the others. "Can I be Goldilocks?"

Christopher cannot resist Mollie's vision of him. "But they didn't see the three bears yet," he says, "because they went to find Goldilocks." He looks at Mollie. "You could be Goldilocks, Mollie."

Her voice consistently comes through to him. She sees the world as a hospitable place where everyone and everything is supposed to fit together, and fantasy is the most dependable glue. Mollie seldom allows an opportunity to escape. "Say it's the same kind like Erik," she tells me, certain that Christopher too must respond to her need to find deeper connections to other children.

20

Mollie knows that Christopher is willing to help another child. When he comes to Sybil's aid at the story table, Mollie is not at all surprised, but I, lacking faith, am astonished.

Sybil has finally placed herself on the story list, but the words will not come. Silently, she stares at Christopher who plays with colored rods in the seat next to her.

"What's your story about, Sybil?" I ask.

"I don't know," she whispers.

"It's about Sybil," Christopher says, not looking up.

"Is it, Sybil?"

She nods her head.

"What do you do in the story?"

"I don't know."

"She goes for a walk," Christopher answers for her again. "I'm making a piano. Don't touch this, Sybil." He is creating a design that will soon cover a third of the table. Mollie watches him as he develops his piano and Sybil's story at the same time.

Christopher examines Sybil. "Do you want the girl to see a elephant? Do you want her to ride on the elephant? Do you want them to play?"

Mollie calls to Erik. "Erik, hurry. Look at Christopher. He's making a piano. A real one."

"So what. I can make six pianos," he says, coming to see what Christopher has done. A number of children crowd around as Christopher completes a recognizable keyboard. More impressive to me is the fact that he recognized Sybil's dilemma and helped her tell a story.

The next morning, however, he behaves as if neither accomplishment took place. When I ask him to show Adam how to make a piano, he builds instead a tower of orange rods. Similarly, he denies any connection between Sybil's story and the one he is about to tell. He will not give up his separateness so casually, in the guise of performing good deeds. It is real connections he is after.

"An elephant and a girl," he dictates.

"Is this like the story you helped Sybil tell?"

"Not a girl. An elephant and a bear."

"What do they do?"

"Nothing."

Upstairs, I read Christopher's story. "An elephant and a bear. They do nothing."

"Are they in the zoo?" Erik asks Christopher.

"Yeah."

"That's why they don't do nothing."

Christopher interprets Erik's interest as a sign of friendship and moves to the seat next to him. When Erik jumps up to volunteer for a part, Christopher copies him.

"Can I be the lion, Libby?"

"Can I be the lion, Libby?" Christopher echoes.

The storytellers choose Erik, but Christopher persists with increasing animation. Then, as I begin Amelia's story about a girl who meets a rabbit in the forest, Christopher is on his feet before Erik can respond.

"Me! Me! I'm first. I'm the rabbit! Me!"

"Okay, Christopher," Amelia says.

He can hardly sit still. He waits for the first characters to be named, then waves his arms wildly. It is as if he has suddenly realized that the characters are already inside the stories, and that he is not the one who puts them there.

"The hippo! Me, me, me! You didn't never pick me!"

The children cannot resist his entreaties. Christopher is given four successive roles as the group watches his excitement with the same interest they give to the stories. He too is part of the unfolding drama of the classroom.

Even Christopher must feel something has changed. Later, when I read "The Lion and the Rat," he is uncharacteristically confident as he comments on the story.

"The lion hasta do that," he says.

"Do what?"

"Grow bigger to have sharp teeth. He's the lord of the jungle. The rat don't do that."

"Oh, you mean the lion should have chewed through the net, not the rat?"

"Because he's the lord of the jungle, and he shouldn't have stepped where the net is."

"Those other animals wasn't nice to the lion," Maria says. "They didn't help him."

"That's because they're *not* the lord of the jungle," Christopher states definitively.

21

I have asked Christopher's parents to bring him to school early for a while. They are not surprised by his school problems because his behavior at home is of concern to them as well.

"What will he be doing if he comes early?"

"Nothing special. Mollie is here and so are a few others. With a smaller group, it's easier to become involved in good play."

Mollie is finishing the third wall of a block house when Christopher arrives. "Hey, Christopher? Do you want to sit inside my mousie hole?"

He looks around, puzzled. "Where did the children go?"

"When it's your birthday everyone comes early," Mollie says. Her reply confuses me until I realize that apparently she did not understand it was she who was *late* on the day of her birthday.

Mollie repeats her invitation. "Hurry up. Come in the mousie hole, Christopher."

Christopher, already at the easel, pays no attention to Mollie. "Are you my friend, Christopher?" she yells, exasperatedly. "Yes or no!"

"Yes."

"Then you have to sleep in my mousie place right now this minute."

He stops painting and joins Mollie. She rarely gives ultimatums, but she and Margaret have begun to play "Yes or no?" and "Are you or aren't you?" when they are alone; Christopher is now in the category of special friends with whom to practice her growing repertoire of social expressions.

"You are or you aren't," Mollie says to Christopher. "Are you or aren't you a elephant? Do you want to be a baby elephant comes to see the baby mousie in the hole?"

"I'm the daddy."

"I'm the mommy. Goodnight, daddy mousie. Go to sleep, don't bite."

"Goodnight. Go to sleep."

"Wake up, eat your cheese."

"Wake up, eat your beeze."

"If it's hot."

"If it's cold. Hey, Mollie, you want to go for a walk in the woods and see if Goldilocks is coming?"

Maria and Samantha walk in and are surprised to see Christopher. "Hey, Mollie, you wanna make a bigger house? Hey, let's use all the blocks. But not Christopher. He'll knock it down."

"Hold on, girls," I say. "Christopher is playing *with* Mollie. You have to ask them both if you can make the house bigger."

"Can we, Christopher?"

"Yes, if you don't break it down."

"Okay, only three-year-old boys allowed. No four-year-old boys."

"Our house is so nice," Maria says, piling on more blocks.

"Our house is the best house," Samantha agrees. "It's the only house you can have fun and diamonds and gold in."

Erik has come in quietly. "It's a dumb house," he says. "Nobody can make a motor home but me."

Christopher jumps out of the house. "Me too, Erik. I'm Erik too. Call me Erik."

"You are not, dum-dum. I'm Erik."

"I'm Erik. That's my Purple Panther."

"It's not a Purple Panther. It's He-Man. And it's mine. Keep your hands off!"

"Purple Panther, Purple Panther."

"I'm going to cut off your head if you keep saying that."

"Erik, please. Don't get so mad," I say, stepping between the boys. "Christopher, it *is* He-Man and it belongs to Erik."

"Mine, mine. I'm Erik too."

"Come on, Christopher, stop. We'll get all mixed up if you call yourself Erik."

Christopher runs to the playdough table and pushes a large pile on the floor. "Stop, Christopher. Look at the mess." He closes his eyes and falls limply against my legs. "Hey, Christopher, what's wrong? You were playing so nicely with Mollie before. Did the big children upset you?"

"No."

"Look, Mollie's in the doll corner now. Let's see what she's doing. What are you children playing?"

"We're having pumpkin soup," Mollie says.

"Ask if you can play, Christopher."

"Can I play?"

"Oh, nice, Christopher. How nice," Margaret says in a grown-up voice. "I'll pour you some mint tea."

"Mommy, mommy," Barney whines. "I'm too hungry. Feed me, feed me."

"Here's food, baby. Eat this. Too hot. Don't burn your fingers."

"Don't burn your nose," Christopher says.

"Don't burn your toes," Mollie rhymes. "Don't burn your clothes, baby boze."

"Daddy, daddy. Hurry up. Hello? Hello? Who's the daddy?"

"Christopher is the daddy. Cover him up, daddy."

"Okay. Go to sleep, little baby."

Christopher's voice blends with the others until I can barely distinguish between the speakers. Then Mollie's tone changes:

"Don't say you're Erik, Christopher," she says sternly. "*Don't* say that, *ever!*"

"Why?"

"Because his mommy will be angry at you. She'll put you to bed without your supper. Just say you're Christopher. Or say you're the daddy."

Suddenly Mollie perceives the difference between playing a role and declaring yourself to be another child who exists in real life. The first is proper; you can be yourself or play a fictional role, both of which are acceptable realities. The idea of taking the persona of someone in the class falls into no recognizable category, but it feels wrong and is therefore punishable by going to bed without supper.

22

"It's a Peter and the Wolf," Mollie says, settling down into the first story of the day. "I'm Peter and the wolf. I mean . . . I'm Peter and . . . I'm going to be 'and the wolf.' " She cannot decide if "and the" belongs with Peter or with the wolf.

"Am I in your story, Mollie?" Erik asks, even before he hangs up his coat.

"You're Peter and the Wolf," Mollie says.

"Not Peter. I'll be the wolf."

"No, Erik. *I'm* the wolf. You're Peter."

"I won't be Peter. If I can't be the wolf, I won't be in your dumb story."

"We can both be the wolf. Is that a nice thing?"

"Never mind. I'll be Sasha. She's the bird."

Erik relaxes the moment Mollie offers a compromise. But why should he care so much about Mollie's story? She is three and he is nearly five. I can imagine only that he feels particularly vulnerable this morning and needs immediate compensation. Mollie is the first available person with something to give.

The table fills up as Mollie begins. "They saw a wolf going behind the tree. And then the wolf climbed up the tree and scared them. Not the grandfather because he's inside sleeping. And they both go home and have supper."

"Who are 'they,' Mollie?" I ask.

"Peter and the wolf and Sasha."

"Peter and Sasha?"

"Peter and the. . . . Sasha."

"I'm telling that one too," Barney decides. "But mine has hunters. And then the hunters banged the drum. Peter climbed up the tree and tied a rope on the wolf."

Stuart is next. I am fairly certain he will carry on the Peter and the Wolf theme, because he and Barney are frequently inspired by Mollie's stories.

"Mine is different, Mollie," he says. "Mine has the wolf banged on the drum. And then Peter says, 'What are you doing, Mr. Wolf? Mr. Wolf, what are you banging?'"

Libby's story is different in another way, for she must always include a little girl. "There was a wolf in the forest. And then Peter came and saw the little girl. Then they climbed up the tree and banged on the drum and the wolf ran away. Samantha and Amelia are the hunters when they found us."

"I was before Libby," Erik says, pushing a chair between mine and Libby's. "You forgot to write my name. I'm Han Solo. Then Darth Vader tries to kill Han Solo but Han Solo knocks him down. The Darth kills Han but he didn't really kill him. So he throws all the rocks on the moon at Darth Vader."

"Why did he do that, Erik?" Mollie asks.

"Do what?"

"Throw all the rocks on the moon at Darth Vader."

"Because he's a bad guy. Han Solo is a good guy."

"Oh." She turns to Margaret. "Did you hear that? Don't you think that's very, very, very interesting? And guess what, Margaret? At cleanup time, I gave Erik two blocks to carry and he said, 'Thank you, Mollie.'" She flushes with excitement, but Margaret frowns.

"You don't know how to make an S," she tells Mollie, who bursts into tears. "She said I can't make an S, teacher. She's a liar," Mollie cries, using one of Libby's favorite expressions.

"Why are you crying, Mollie?" Christopher asks.

"Margaret said I can't make an S."

"Don't say that, Margaret," he says, sharply.

"I can, too."

"I say no! And I'm not putting you in my story."

"Okay, I won't say it."

Christopher has tried out the mock threat and negotiated settlement – and it works. He looks at Margaret in surprise. She seldom asks to be in his stories but, put this way, it is an offer she cannot refuse.

23

The stories flow in unbounded variety and no first-time story is the same as any other. The three-year-olds listen to the daily accumulation of stories, but when the spirit finally moves the new storyteller, it is invariably a unique event.

What determines the choice of subject, I often wonder. Sometimes, as in the case of Fredrick's water stories, an unforgettable trauma is brought into view. At other times, a chance glimpse at objects on the table becomes the focus for a story: "A crayon. A marker. A string."

"What happened to you in the water?" I may ask. Or, "What is done with the crayon, marker, and string?" If the child is ready, the image is taken a step further; otherwise, the story remains as is: an idea waiting for action.

Most first stories, however, lie somewhere between the compulsory and the accidental. They refer to scenes that are not overwhelming but need to be played out again. Mollie's first story, for example, dealt with the bad guys she heard about in school.

"About a bad guy and a horse. The robbers and the horse. He takes things away from the girl."

Here are some other first stories dictated by this year's three-year-olds:

"Batman goes whoosh. In the Batmobile" (Barney).

"The gorilla gets out of the cage" (William).

"The mommy walks and eats and takes a nappie" (Stuart).

"Me finds a train. And the trains stopped. And the trains sleeped" (Edward).

"Doggie. Woof-woof. My doggie. He's not bad" (Emily).

"Five kitty cats run away. Superman pows them away" (Sybil).

"The mouse goes up the clock. Then he runs down and cuts a hole to sit in" (Margaret).

As storytelling expands, its social dimensions are discovered, and here too the stamp of individuality is remarkable. William, at one end of the continuum, allows no one to enter his stories. "The boy goes fast faster faster in his racing car," he says, rolling the car along the edge of the table. When he acts out the story, his pleasure arises from being watched as he zooms his car around the rug.

Fredrick, on the other hand, has learned to use his stories as social insurance: "The first navigator sits with the pilot up in front and helps him drive," his story begins, but, once upstairs, he continually interrupts with new directions that bring more actors to the stage.

"Wait, there's a second navigator too. That's John. He helps me drive."

"Then we'll include John," I agree. "The second navigator also helps the pilot drive."

"No, see, it's a special cockpit that the driver sits up in front. With the good guy. That's Erik."

"So, the driver sits up in a special cockpit with the good guy," I repeat.

"No! They don't sit in the cockpit. Only if they're bad guys. The bad guys—Barney, you're the bad guy—they sit in their special cockpit they try to shoot down the plane but they can't. Adam, you're a bad guy too. Try to shoot me but only pretend, okay? P-too! P-too! And then me and Erik – sit here, Erik – we fly away. Whooshsh!"

Margaret, somewhere between William and Fredrick, makes her doll the heroine but then watches the audience reaction so closely that certain children feel compelled to help.

"Cabbage Patch comes. Then a wolf comes. Then she is scared. She runs away." The wolf, who is Margaret, howls modestly and looks around.

"No, Margaret!" Adam blurts out. "The wolf howls like this. ROARRR! Let me be the wolf because I really know how they howl."

"Let me be the mother that picks her up," Libby offers.

"No, I'm the mother that hasta pick her up," Margaret whispers, hugging Cabbage Patch. "You be the sister that picks her up. And then it's summer and she goes out to play." Again, Margaret peers about, waiting.

"But doesn't she meet the wolf again?" Erik asks. "Before you went out didn't the wolf hided by the other side of your house and he came out and he scared you again?"

"Yes."

My turn: Does Cabbage Patch run away or does she do something different this time?

Margaret hesitates only a moment. "She scares the wolf away. Then she goes out to play."

"With me?" Mollie suggests, rising hopefully from her seat.

"Yes."

Even more singular than subject and style are the symbols each class develops. Barney introduces a new stage prop, a simple idea, yet one I have seen in no other group. He prints the letter D on a small piece of paper and creates a story in order to use it.

"Spiderman steps on a D. Then R2D2 steps on a D. Then C3PO steps on a D."

Upstairs the older children give more substance to the D.

"If you step on a D," Erik suggests, "you fall in a trap."

"And you get out with a ladder," Libby adds.

"Yeah, a ladder," Barney agrees. He is pleased by the metamorphosis of his idea. For the remainder of the term, the D – which is sometimes another letter but is referred to as "Barney's D" – is used to trap people and get them out of traps with ladders.

The following year, with Barney still in the class, the D is remembered but seldom used. The cultural artifacts of a class are the products of a single group at a specific time and usually nontransferable.

One day at snack time Mollie asks Barney if he has his D. "I didn't tell a story today," he answers. The D exists only in stories, but in Mollie's mind it is a part of his school persona.

"We all know Barney's D," I say. "What about Stuart? Does he put something special in *his* stories?"

"He's a train!"

"And Mollie?"

"A ghost and a wolf."

"Margaret is a kitty."

"So is Carrie. And William is a bunny."

"Christopher's a elephant."

"I'm the Hulk," Fredrick says proudly.

"Erik is good guys and bad guys," Christopher says. "And He-Man."

The snack table conversation is purposeful and accurate, for it is natural to picture one another in play roles. By contrast, in a general discussion held later in the day, the same children completely miss the point and substitute an irrelevant fantasy for social policy.

"There was a lot of arguing in the blocks today," I begin, "and we must talk about it. Tulio and Peter used up all the blocks and no one else could build."

"Erik does it too," Tulio says.

"I know, and so do others. What should we do about it?"

"Just give the other people that don't have any about nine or eleven blocks," Libby says.

"No, three or four, or six or seven," Erik advises, "or ten is enough."

Fredrick jumps up. "If somebody comes in the school and gets five or ten, then when the lights are off, they'll get scared."

"When will the lights be off, Fredrick?" I ask.

"He means when a kid turns them off," John explains.

"We'll keep the lights on. Now, Tulio, next time what will you do if someone needs blocks and you've used them all?"

"Give Libby nine blocks."

Mollie speaks directly to Fredrick. "If you turn two lights out then you can't see because it's dark and you could be scared of monsters."

"We'll keep all the lights on, Mollie," I assure her.

"If I use all the blocks, I'll give ninety-eight to Libby," Samantha says.

"Or to anyone else who wants to build," I say.

"If the birds eat the blocks then people can't have any."

"We're not talking about birds, Barney," Erik says. "Just listen. Give people ten blocks. That's it. Ten."

"If you turn off the light and then you turn *on* the light, that kid'll get scared."

"And he'll go away?" Mollie asks Fredrick, who cannot abandon his idea.

"If a birdie comes in, he won't have any blocks," Barney decides. "And not the kid either."

"Here's a good idea," Adam states. "If you take all the blocks, give back every *kind*, not just small ones. Big ones, too. About seventeen."

The older children recite numbers while the threes are distracted by images of dark rooms and intrusive birds. In either case there is no improvement in subsequent block play. Those who rushed to capture the block supply continue to do so; enforced counting seems to encourage greed, not communal spirit. As Adam predicted, the children keep the bigger blocks and count out the four-inch size.

Within a few days, by unspoken consent, the children revert to the old ways whereby fantasy, not numbers, is the measuring tool. You are more inclined to share blocks when you share fantasies.

Several morning later, Mollie says to Christopher, "Where are those birds?"

He looks around the block area. "They didn't come yet."

"Oh, yeah. That's when the kid turns off the light."

"You know, Mollie," I say. "There *is* no kid who turns off the lights, or any birds who come in our room. We were talking about not taking too many blocks."

"And the birds can't have any."

Mollie cannot envision "too many blocks" since she has little sense of how many she uses when she builds. She can, however, imagine a bird stealing blocks or a ghost taking the little girl's pies. The sense of wrongdoing comes across in the fantasy long before block area logistics are unraveled.

24

I discover that it is easier to correct a bird's image than to explain a new riddle game.

"I have a game," I say at snack time. "Try to guess what animal I'm thinking about. It flies around outside and does not fly into our classroom."

"A bird!"

"And it does not bother our blocks."

"A bird!"

"Good. Now here's another. It's very big and has a long nose that reaches to the ground."

"Elephant!"

"Right. Now who can give us a different animal to guess? Tell us something about the animal and we have to guess the name."

"A wolf!" Mollie shouts. "Mine goes fast as a wolf. It's a wolf."

"Mine goes going down the sides a long nose called an elephant," Barney says.

"But you're not letting us guess. Listen to how I do it. I'm thinking of an animal that swims at the zoo and goes clap, clap with its flappers. But I can't tell you the name. You have to guess."

"Why?" Emily asks.

"It's a game. Like in the riddle book. You don't find out the answer until you turn the page, remember? Well, in this game you don't give the name of the animal until people try to guess what it is."

"A lion," Stuart says. "He roars."

"A giraffe!"

Mollie is excited. "*My* favorite animal is tiger a leopard an animal a zebra with red stripes and black stripes."

"It has black stripes a zebra," Fredrick answers.

"Did you guess, Fredrick?" Mollie asks.

"Yeah."

Clearly my expectations are unrealistic. To delay naming the animal makes no sense; it is the opposite of accepted practice in fantasy play where identification comes first. "You're the cat" precedes "meow-meow." The riddle game should be postponed for a later date. However, the next day Mollie tells us she is thinking of a bear the moment she sits down at the snack table. I have no choice but to try again to teach the game.

"What does the bear look like, Mollie?"

"Big brown it's furry."

"All right. This is the way to make a riddle. Mollie is thinking of something that is big and brown and furry. What is it?"

"A bear!"

"Me! Now *I'm* thinking," Margaret says. "A elephant."

" No, a walrus."

"What does it look like, Stuart?"

"A tail with fat hands."

"Stuart is thinking of an animal with a tail and fat hands."

"A walrus!"

"A walrus. I said it first!"

Their riddles remind me of the game Mollie plays with Christopher.

"Say 'table.' "

"Table."

"Say 'chair.' "

"Chair."

"Now you tell me to say it."

The children take over the riddle game and develop their own rituals. They begin each session with the same animals: Mollie calls out a bear, Stuart a walrus, and Margaret an elephant. Then someone says, "Guess what?" and they all shout, "Bear! Walrus! Elephant!"

After a few days, I attempt to alter the pattern. "This is not an animal. I'm thinking of a piece of furniture. It's very hard wood, with four legs, and we put food on it."

"A horse!"

"Wait, there's more. We put glasses on it and a juice pitcher."

"Orange juice!"

"Apple juice!"

"Here's another clue. We put crackers in a basket on the . . .?"

"Saltines!"

Before I can figure out why my clues are so confusing, Christopher says, "It has a green mark on it."

"The table!"

"It's where I sit," I say, taking his cue.

"The chair!"

"I go to sleep in there," Carrie says.

"That's your bed," replies Christopher, who then gives another riddle of his own. "Something you put in. It's a mouth."

"Mine is soft on my head," Mollie offers.

"A pillow."

Suddenly everyone understands the game. Christopher points to his shirt. "It gots on it Superman."

"Superman shirt. Did I guess it?" Fredrick asks. "Hey, you wanna play Superman? I'm Batman."

"I'm the mother," Mollie says, and the real game begins. "Pretend it's morning."

"Pour the tea," Margaret demands. "Tea, tea, I want tea."

"Give the baby tea," Batman says.

"All gone."

"All gone."

"Riki-tiki-tomi."

"Riki-tiki-tomi."

My games consistently miss the point of *their* games: the recognition and repetition of what is obvious to all. The threes have been demonstrating these facts to me for months, but I keep adding complications. A few days later the unadorned simplicity of it all comes across to me.

We are playing an invention of mine called "Who's missing, who's missing, guess who's not here," in which one child hides behind a screen while another child tries to guess his identity. The fours play the game easily, giving appropriate hints and not peeking. I cannot, however, convince the threes to observe two important rules: do not reveal the hidden person's name and, if you are the one who is hiding, do not come out before your name is guessed.

Suddenly I see the game through younger eyes. "Let's play a different way," I tell the children. "We'll all watch the hider, we'll pretend we don't know who it is, and then we'll all say who it is."

We sing the original refrain, changing the last line to suit the new rules: "Who's missing, who's missing, guess who's not here. It's Mollie, it's Mollie, now she is here."

Together we watch Mollie hide and after a moment of closing our eyes we call out her name. Mollie jumps out laughing. "It's me!"

The new game is a splended success, not unlike the three-year-olds' hide-and-seek, in which they pretend to hide and pretend to seek. Carrie has her own version: she hides a favorite possession, then asks a teacher to help her find it. She pretends to look for it as she takes the teacher directly to the missing item. "Oh, here's my dolly's brush!" she squeals delightedly. All these games resist the unknown and the possibility of loss. They are designed to give the child control in the most direct way.

Sometimes, however, the child has no control; something is really missing. Then the threes are likely to approach the problem as if the question is "What is *not* missing?" This is exactly what happens when I try to direct the children's attention to an empty space in the playground. Over the weekend, an unsafe climbing structure has been removed. The doll corner window overlooks the area that housed the rickety old frame.

"See if you can tell what's missing from our playground?" I ask.

"The sandbox."

"The squirrely tree."

"The slide."

"But I can *see* all those things. They're still in the playground. Something else was there, something very big, and now it's gone."

"The boat."

"Mollie, look. There's the boat. I'm talking about a big, brown, wooden thing that was right there where my finger is pointing."

"Because there's too much dirt."

"But what was on top of the place where there's too much dirt?"

"It could be grass. You could plant grass."

Libby and Samantha see us crowded around the window and walk over to investigate. "Where's the climbing house?" Libby asks. "Someone stoled the climbing house."

"No one stole the house, Libby. We asked some men to take it down for us. Remember how shaky it was? We were afraid somebody would fall."

The threes continue staring, confused. I should have anticipated their response and urged that the structure be dismantled during school hours. After all, these are the children who scrub a clean table because it had playdough on it the day before, and worry about birds coming in to bother the blocks.

"Does everyone remember the climbing house? Here, I'll draw a picture. Let's see, it went up this high and here were some steps . . . "

"Where are the steps?" Mollie asks.

"The men chopped everything up and took it all away in a truck."

"Where are they stepping to?"

"The steps are not steps any more. I'll bet they're using all the old wood for firewood."

"They use them to step out of the fire," Mollie says.

"Like the D!" Barney exclaims. There is a moment of recognition and smiles all around. With Barney's symbol of change, the children can avoid the disturbing image of a missing stairway and think instead of magical escapes they have acted out many times.

25

Mollie's riddle-making takes a new turn; she looks into her own experience and begins to use riddles as another way of explaining herself to children. "I'm thinking of something you have to be a girl if you're not a girl you can't tie a pink ribbon in your hair."

"A pink ribbon."

"Two ribbons," Mollie says, fingering her new ponytails. My original elephant example is still invoked, but the children are more innovative since I stopped contributing ideas.

"It's a thing so you turn so you could get in the house and it's a knob." This is Emily's third doorknob riddle.

Christopher has a new one. "When it's dark you can see a monster coming there. A ghost."

"I'm thinking of something you have to be a girl," Mollie says again. "If you're not a girl you can't tie a pink ribbon in your hair."

"Two pink ribbons!" No one tells Mollie she is repeating herself; her riddle is appreciated even more the second time.

"No. Only one pink ribbon because I'm hiding the other one in my hand."

Everyone laughs. Mollie has grown confident in her ability to interest children in her ideas. Therefore she is all the more hurt later in the blocks when her notions of number and space are questioned.

"Teacher, Mollie is taking my blocks!" Margaret complains.

"She has too much than I have," Mollie pouts, examining her large collection, which is at least twice the size of Margaret's.

"Not more. Only four more," Margaret argues. Neither girl can judge the relative size of their structures.

"But, Mollie, you already have more than Margaret."

"No I don't." Mollie's eyes fill at my suggestion that she is wrong. Were I to invoke the block-eating birds as the cause of uneven block distribution, the girls would instantly have a believable explanation.

"Perhaps you both need more blocks. There are some over there no one is using."

"But Margaret has to give me nine blocks." She remembers the unused rule but cannot see that her friend has fewer than nine blocks in her entire building.

"Margaret doesn't have enough to share this time, Mollie. Take some from the shelf, why don't you?"

"Let's play in the doll corner, okay, Margaret?" Mollie suggests, satisfied that justice has prevailed. Before I can leave, however, another controversy explodes and, once again, it has more to do with physical perception than social readiness.

"He's making his blocks go on my ship!" Barney screams. "I keep telling him not to."

"I'm making a ship, too," Stuart says.

"Why not connect your ships?"

"I don't want to," Barney says.

"Well, then, could you build your ship in *that* direction, Stuart? You'll have more room if you do."

Stuart nods, then places two more blocks against Barney's ship. "See, he's doing it again!"

"Stuart, can you put those four blocks at the other end? Then it won't bump into Barney's ship."

"I am. That's what I'm doing."

"See if you can help him, Barney. He's having trouble doing it."

"Okay, I'll do it for him." Barney starts to rearrange the blocks only to find himself retracing Stuart's steps. The two boys can no more change the direction of the existing structure than control the lines they draw on a piece of paper.

Automatically I think of Christopher. What if he too cannot direct himself away from another person's boundary lines? Yet he is the only three-year-old boy who has good control over lines and shapes. Social boundaries and linear design must require entirely different kinds of perception.

"Christopher, can you come help Stuart? He wants to turn his spaceship around so it doesn't bump into Barney's."

Christopher, who has been playing alone on the window seat, sizes up the problem and in four quick moves changes the direction of the protruding wall. Unhampered by social considerations he solves the problem of boundaries with ease. Clearly, when he climbs all over another child's territory, it is not because he does not visualize its dimensions.

The boys are surprised by Christopher's accomplishment but Christopher himself is not impressed. At three an early skill does not always carry with it the conscious awareness of achievement if it is not used to further a fantasy. Since Christopher had no role in the space odyssey, he could not *imagine* himself as a man big and powerful enough to change the direction of a spaceship.

"Christopher, come here!" Mollie calls from the doll corner. "Pretend you're talking to me. Who's this? Say, 'Who's this?'"

"Who's this?"

"Hello, is this Jacob?"

"This is Jacob."

"No, say, 'Who's this?'"

"Who's this?"

"This is Jacob's mother. Where is Jacob?"

"He's asleep."

"Oh, that's why. Okay, go to bed, Jacob."

"Am I Jacob?"

"No, you're the father. It's Jacob's birthday. I'm making him a pie."

Waves of high-pitched voices roll through the doorway singing of birthdays and babies, of telephone calls and pies in the oven. Tiny arguments, more for practice than purpose, provide the necessary counterpoint.

"That's mine!"

"It's mine first."

"Tell the teacher."

"Tell his mother."

"Call the doctor. Hello? Hello? Is this Jacob? Are you sick?"

"Call me Superman, Mollie."

"Hello, hello, is this Superman?"

"Yeah. I'll be right back. I need to fly for five minutes."

Christopher runs through the room, arms aloft, coming to a halt at Stuart's spaceship. "I'm Superman," he tells the boys. "Do you see any trouble?"

"There was a robber here trying to steal our bullets."

"Okay. I'll catch the bad guy." Christopher's look of self-awareness was not evident when he rebuilt Stuart's ship. He completes a quick swoop around the blocks and then flies back into the doll corner where Mother is slicing the birthday pie.

26

"Are you still the father?" Mollie asks Christopher.

"I'm a bad guy now. I'm the bad Superman."

"No you're not."

"Yes I am!" Christopher picks up the nearest doll and throws it on the floor. For the first time he feels strong enough to oppose Mollie. "I banged your baby!"

"Stop that. You can't play, Christopher."

He runs to the window seat and knocks the row of animals over with the giraffe. "Bang you, bang you, down you go," he says softly. "The bad giraffe pushes the zebra. Watch out. Here he comes. Look out, look out."

Christopher carefully stands the animals back into neat formation, then sweeps through them again with the bad giraffe. He is too absorbed to notice the mounting excitement behind him in the block area.

"We're magic girls," Samantha tells Amelia. "Get those big blocks. We can be Wonderwoman."

"Let's live with Erik. Ask him."

"Can we live in the same place, Erik?"

"Yeah. Superman and Wonderwoman and Batman. But I'm Luke."

"Who's Robin?"

"Me, me! I said first!" Fredrick jumps around in front of Erik. "I'm Robin, okay? Can I be?"

"Yeah. You gotta make the Batmobile."

"Hey, Luke," Libby says to Erik, "we have to stop the bad guys. I see Batman's not alive."

"Yeah, he's alive. He's in his Batmobile."

"Hey, Luke, I forgot to tell you," Libby says. "I have a baby. This is Wonderwoman's house. I need you to take care of the baby, Luke. You're my husband."

"I forgot, I can't play now, Libby. I gotta paint a picture. C'mon, John. My mother told me to paint a picture today."

Libby looks distraught. "Fredrick, are you still Robin? Are you my son? We need a Batman. Hey, Christopher, you want to be our husband? You want to be Batman?"

Christopher looks up in surprise. He gathers his animals and steps into Wonderwoman's house.

"Don't bring those in! We don't need those!"

"It's Star Wars," he says.

"We're not playing Star Wars. This is Wonderwoman's house."

He picks up several animals and throws them at Fredrick who catches the tiger and laughs. "Good throw, you dum-dum. Hey, you wanna play tiger? Pretend we're having a fight. My tiger pushes your elephant, okay?"

"Except don't let the tiger win," Christopher says, getting inside the Batmobile. For a few moments, the boys butt their animals and make growling noises. Then, without warning, Christopher grabs the tiger and returns to the window seat.

"Give it back, Christopher! That's my tiger!" Fredrick rushes to the window seat and punches Christopher on the back. "I'm Masters of the Universe! You're dead!" he yells, running away.

"You better stop that, Fredrick! I'm telling the teacher."

He watches Fredrick disappear into the cubby room, then sits down among the fallen animals. "The baby elephant comes to the house," he whispers. "The mother didn't come to the daddy yet. The daddy elephant bumps the giraffe and he falls down. Stop that I'm telling and he falls in the water and he swims away. Where's the teacher?"

He finds me at the painting table. "Fredrick hit me. On my back. He punched me."

"Why did he do that?"

"I don't know."

I call Fredrick over. "Why did you hit him?"

"Because he took the tiger without asking."

"Okay, you're both wrong. Fredrick, don't hit, and Christopher, don't grab."

"Next time," Christopher tells me, "I won't give him the tiger and then, if he wants it back, he has to ask me. Hey, Erik, can I see your He-Man?"

"No."

Christopher walks away, then turns around quickly and punches Erik twice on his arm.

"Cut that out, you!"

"Show me your He-Man."

"No. I said no. And if you do that again I'll throw you in the river."

"Like the troll?"

"Yeah, like the troll."

"Then you're the biggest billy goat, Erik."

"Okay, I'm the biggest billy goat. Crunch! Crunch!"

"Hey, Erik, pretend I'm the troll, okay? Who's that walking over my bridge?"

"It's me, the biggest billy goat," Erik answers.

"Then I'm coming to gobble you up!" roars Christopher. "Gr-r-r!"

"No you don't! I'll knock out your brains and butt you in the water!" Erik lowers his head and pretends to push Christopher who flops on the floor and swims away.

Miraculously, Christopher has salvaged the scene. One scene is not the entire play, but it is a beginning. Having started a fight, he substitutes a fantasy for the real aggression. Furthermore, it is *his* fantasy, not Mollie's. She can support him and play with him, but she cannot speak for him.

27

Often I must disconnect myself from the tableau. A mixture of dissonance and harmony moves around the classroom, the crises in one place offset by a peaceful scene in another. The children flex their social muscles and test the environment. Are they safe enough in this classroom to say and do these things, and, when they've had enough, can they stop? The boys sound more often as if real trouble is brewing, but their disguises fool me, not the other children.

"Blow that house up, John."

"Do you have a gun? Should I make you one?"

"He's shot. One-two-three-blast off!"

"We gotta kill some bad guys."

"Pow! Pow! You're dead."

"I'm the bad guy. And then the bad guy beats the good guy up."

"Then the good guy jumps up and knocks the bad guy's head off."

"Put the bombs on. Those are bombs, right?"

"I'm a bad Superman."

"I'm a good Superman."

"But, John, I'm going to be a bad Superman. Aren't you?"

"Okay, I'm bad, too. No, I mean, I'm still good."

"Look, John, what if you say you want to be a good guy? Say you were still my friend and I say I want to be a bad guy Superman and you say, you can say, 'I want to be a good guy Superman,' 'cause the other person could tell you when you're not your friend."

"Well, Erik, I'm going to be a good Superman but I'm still going to be your friend."

"But just be a bad Superman, can't you? Because I'm going to be one. C'mon, can't you, John?"

"See, good really means bad. See, if I say good it really means *bad*."

"Okay, we're bad, but we still could kill the bad guys, okay? Hey, Mollie, get off. You can't come on this place. It's deadly poison. One step and you'll die."

"Can you tie my shoe, John?"

"Okay. Wait a minute, Erik. I have to tie Mollie's shoe."

"Margaret's not my friend, John," Mollie says, watching him struggle with her laces.

"Why not?"

"She's Emily's friend."

"Hey, Mollie, ask Mrs. Paley to do this. Something is wrong with the shoelaces."

"Mrs. Paley, tie my shoes, please. Margaret's not my friend. Did you know?"

"Why do you think she's not?"

"She's Emily's friend. I want to tell a wolf story, for Chinese things and red things." Mrs. Alter and I have been taping up red streamers that say "Happy New Year" in Chinese. Mollie's wolf story is not exactly Chinese, but one holiday makes a suitable stand-in for another in preschool.

"Once upon a time there was a little girl and she made a valentine. And then another girl Chinese came and made circles. And the wolf came and made valentines *and* circles. It's a Chinese story for Emily."

"She's not in your story," Margaret says. "She's in *my* story, not yours. I writed my own story." Margaret shows me a piece of paper covered with wavy lines. "We're Superman. Me and Emily."

"Superman's not a girl," Mollie snaps. "He's a man. And *I'm* a wolf. And you're not in *my* story. My story is about the three pigs and you're not in there, Margaret. And you're going to be in big trouble!"

"I'm not trouble!" Margaret shouts.

Mollie backs down. "Okay, you could be in my story. Are you my friend?"

"No."

"Well, I'm Emily's friend."

"No, because I'm Margaret's friend," Emily says.

"Well, anyway, Emily, I'm Mollie's friend," Margaret states. "She's Supergirl and Emily is the mother and Mollie is the big sister and Wonderwoman." The girls hold hands and march into the doll corner, ready to play best friends until the next eruption. It comes quickly, as if the girls need to pretend to argue in order to understand more clearly what is happening when they are really angry.

"I want that for me," Emily pouts, pulling a blue negligee away from Margaret. "I brought this dress for me!"

"Stop fighting, Emily," Mollie says.

"But I brought this for me and she brought that for her. We're not fighting, aren't we? No, we're not fighting. Aren't we are not fighting, Margaret?"

"Right. We're not fighting. No fighting in this class."

"We're not fighting," Mollie repeats. "No. Because we're never going to fight in this day. That kitty is fighting. Not us, right?"

"Right. Meow, meow. No! No! I told you one hundred times don't play with the baby's toys, you bad kitty."

"No fighting in this class, kitty. Go to your room!"

"I told my baby not to cry. Thirty times."

"Wait, that's *my* baby!"

"No! I picked it up!"

"Stop fighting. Stop fighting."

"Okay, Mommy. We're never going to fight the whole day. The whole thirty hundred hours."

The angry-sister skit leaves a good aftertaste and the girls are quick to repeat the performance the next day. However, following a few choruses of "Stop fighting—we're not fighting" the emphasis suddenly changes and deeper feelings are tested.

"Stop saying that, Mommy. I hate you, Mom. No, I don't."

"Ding-a-ling. Time to get up, sisters."

"No fair. I hate you, Mom. I mean, I hate that breakfast."

"Yeah, that's the kind we hate."

"Here's some cookies then."

"I don't like it."

"I hate it. You're a bad mother."

"I am not! You're a bad child!"

"Okay, you're a good mother."

"Pretend you're still bad and I say, 'Go to your room and lock the door.'"

"But really we're very good, right?"

The quarrels, real and pretend, seem endless, but peace and contentment are lost and regained in a matter of moments as Maria and Amelia demonstrate at the playdough table.

"I can make my brother talk."

"You can't carry him, Maria."

"I can carry him with one hand and you don't know how to."

"Michael will get you. He's a bad guy."

"My dad will throw you in a cupboard where there's ants."

"Oh no he won't."

"He will!"

"I'll tell my daddy on you."

"I'll tell my daddy on *you*."

"My daddy is strong. He'll spank you."

"My dad is strong and *long*. He'll spank *you*."
"Not how hard my dad would spank. My dad is big."
"My dad could punch your eye out."
"I'll put you in a chicken box."
"I'll put *you* in a chicken box."
"I'll put you in a chicken house."
"I'll put you in a chicken mouse."
"One, two, three, four. That's how old you are, Maria."
"I can put little cherries on your cake. Do you want me to, Amelia?"
"Put them all over here. Here, here, here."
"They're so good. Yummy, yummy."
"In my tummy."
The girls smile at each other; the rhyming heralds a peaceful era.

28

Christopher is having a bad day. If John is right, and good means bad, then perhaps it is not a bad day but rather one in which bad feels good. In either case, he is upsetting a lot of people.

"Get out of here, Christopher! Teacher! Come here! He's messin' up our house."

Maria's frustration propels me into action. "I'll help you make your own house, Christopher." I wrap him quickly into a cocoon of blocks, buying ten minutes of quiet, but knowing that a progression of negative acts will follow. I cannot pretend my actions stem from any motives but impatience and lack of faith. Why else would I hurry an expert block builder into a structure he himself did not build?

Christopher's next invasion is into Emily's story. "The kitty runs away . . . "

"Emily is a crocodile."

". . . and the little girl . . . "

"A monster."

"No monster, Christopher," Emily says, surprised.

"The elephant."

"Stop that, Christopher. You're mixing her up on purpose. Let her tell it herself."

Again, I am wrong. My abruptness is more damaging than his words and surely contradicts my belief that storytelling is as much a social skill as a language art. Let Emily decide the merit of his interruptions.

"Emily, do you want Christopher to give you some ideas for your story?" I ask, but he has already moved on to the sand table and begun to knock apart Adam's network of walls.

"Look what you're doing!" Adam shouts, grabbing Christopher and showering him with sand. Christopher wriggles free and runs into the doll corner. I follow him and brush off the sand.

"You made Adam really angry, you know. That's why he got you full of sand. Come on, let's play with playdough."

"I don't want to."

"Are you sad, Christopher?"

"No."

"Do you want to sit on my lap?"

"Yes."

Are Christopher's upheavals so different from other children's, or is it that they are more frequent and unexpected? The children all sit on emotional seesaws, counterrhythms of good and bad feelings running through every activity. Jealousy and contentment, restlessness and calm sweep around the room. "Don't touch this!" becomes "I'm making it for you"; "You can't play" changes to "You wanna build with me?"

The tides are unpredictable. To the adult, the discontent seems too real. I hear myself scolding, lecturing, continually sitting in judgment, but this is exactly what the children want. Every complaint must be taken seriously and dealt with instantly. The verdict is to be pronounced unequivocally so the play can continue. The children do not seek that punishment be inflicted, but they want their moments of indignation recognized and upheld.

"Tulio's taking my blocks!"

"They're mine. He stoled them from me!"

"He pushed me off!"

"I want to sit next to Adam!"

"She says I'm three!"

"You *are* three."

"I don't want her to say it."

This is from Mollie who, though fussy now with a number of children, can usually reestablish the balance quickly. Christopher, on the other hand, moves unilaterally through a conflict, stepping off the seesaw before the other child comes down.

When Libby yells at him for dumping animals into her house, he can think of nothing else to do but throw them at Fredrick. Fortunately, Fredrick does not take offense; he asks Christopher to play tiger, and the situation is saved. If Christopher does initiate a playful response, it is almost accidental, as in the troll and billy goat incident with Erik.

Yet I feel encouraged. Now that Christopher has begun to listen to other children, their rhythms are bound to take hold. Every morning, for example, before the air fills with distractions, Mollie and Margaret demonstrate the technique of ordinary classroom banter:

"I have Pac-Man eyeglasses, Margaret."

"You don't have a Pac-Man shirt, Mollie, and I do."

"Well, I have a one-two-three belt."

"You don't have a Strawberry Shortcake blouse."

"I have Strawberry Shortcake underwear and you don't."

"You don't have a bunk bed."

"I *do* have a bunk bed."

"I have a bigger one."

"Mine is tall and yours is tall, Margaret."

"We *both* have tall beds."

83

The girls vie for control as they search for a common experience. Instead of "Do you have a bunk bed?" they say "I have a bunk bed and you don't." Sometimes they lose faith in the process and we hear a tearful "She says I don't have a bunk bed!" But they would prefer to debate and negotiate, and they work hard to perfect the skills they will need to solve the real problems that arise.

"Margaret, this time I want to be the mother," Mollie whines.

"No, I am."

"You were the other day."

"But Mollie, don't you know? I can't be the mother at home because my sister always is."

"Then when I get to your house I can be?"

"Yes. Tell my sister she could see your Pac-Man eyeglasses."

Christopher does try to enter the ongoing game, now that he realizes there *is* a game, but his syncopation is off. I would gladly teach him the method, if I could, but my rhythms usually don't work either. He must watch the children, find his own style, and practice a great deal. One thing I can do for Christopher is to stop jumping in so quickly. By substituting my own cadence too often, I may be delaying his adaptation to the rhythm of the group.

29

The notion of a group rhythm, intangible and indefinable as it is, makes sense to me. When the children feel at one with the movements and sounds of the room, their creativity and generosity are boundless. They see one another's needs and rush to fill the void, compensating for the times when the world seems out of step.

The antagonisms do not necessarily originate in the classroom. Mollie, for example, is increasingly displeased by her sister's visits. When Leslie was younger and sat in her mother's lap or crawled hesitantly nearby, Mollie kissed her and showered her with toys. Now that Leslie walks around the classroom and takes her own toys, Mollie is unhappy.

"Take her home, Mommy! She can't have that! It belongs to the school."

The visits are less frequent, but Leslie remains on her sister's mind and becomes a factor in her school day. "This is Leslie's cake," Mollie says, pounding the playdough with unusual roughness. "She's eating it all up. Spank the naughty baby, Daddy. She can't come in Mommy's bed."

Margaret portrays her little brother in even darker terms. According to her, Charlie does little else but bite, kick, and scratch when not otherwise occupied with tearing books and damaging pets and appliances.

"Charlie ate the cat."

"Did he get spanked?"

"Yeah, and then he put the cat back and broke the TV."

The girls talk more often about younger siblings than the boys do and act out more scenes involving babies. Mollie is the only girl who refuses to be the baby. She'll be a mother or father, a sister or a cat, but not a baby. "I'm too big to do that," she says.

"I'm bigger than you," Libby argues. "And I'm the baby sometimes."

"Well I don't want to be. Just that's what Leslie has to be."

Mollie deprives herself of a large amount of the comfort given to babies in the doll corner. Emily, preferring the baby's role, receives daily doses of mothering from Libby, Samantha, and Amelia.

"Emily's sad. My baby is sick. Could you come over and play with Emily? She's just a little baby. Like yours."

"My baby is one week old. Is that what Emily is? I'll come rock her to sleep."

"Play with her because she's your baby sister and she's too sad today."

"Baby, I have to hug you. Mommy's going to clean you nice and warm. Tell your mommy."

"Wa-a-ah!"

"Poor baby. Give her everything she wants."

"She wants to go camping. Take all the babies camping this night."

"Me too. With my baby, right?"

"Right. Put on her snuggle bag and hold her tight."

Emily's lot is an enviable one but Mollie is adamant: she will not pretend to be a baby. She wills herself to be bigger, always imagining that she is on the next step. She claimed she could reach her hook before she was able and then, accomplishing that, she insisted she could zip her jacket even as she waited in line for the teacher's help.

"I can tie my shoes, Margaret."

"My big brother ties his shoes with his eyes shut."

"I can do that too."

"Mollie, you *will* be able to tie your shoes when you're older. You and Margaret both."

"I know how already. And I'm building a big, big house. Come on, Margaret. The bad wolf won't blow it down. You can't come in by the hair of my chinney-chin-chin. Then I'll blow and puff your house down. I'm making a wolf house, Margaret."

"Where? I can't see it," Margaret teases, shutting her eyes.

"Turn around, look. This is a strong house."

"Oh, I see it. Can I come in?"

"This is the big bad wolf's house. Get in the side here. Not by the hair of my chinney-chin-chin."

"I came in. I ate you up, Mollie."

Mollie hesitates. "You ate somebody up."

"No, I ate *you* up, Mollie."

"You didn't, because I'm a little girl. This isn't the wolf's house. This is a warm place for two squirrels. We're squirrels. We live in it. I'm the mommy squirrel. You have to be my baby squirrel, Margaret."

"Okay. Here's the squirrely nuts. Cook them in the oven."

Mollie's rhythm is good today. She sidesteps shoe-tying by moving into a wolf's house, and, when the balance in the wolf fantasy appears to topple, she brings in the safe little squirrel family.

Later, when she tells a story, Mollie doesn't have to be quite so nimble since she is in complete command. "It's in the big bad wolf's house. Peter and the wolf had carrots. That was from Mr. McGregor's garden. And the hunters came."

"Is this story about Peter Rabbit, Mollie? Or about Peter and the Wolf?"

"It's about Peter Rabbit *and* Peter and the Wolf. It's the same Peter but it's a different Peter. It's the same wolf but it's a different wolf." By now I am familiar with Mollie's logic: the rabbit and the boy are both called Peter but are different characters in different stories; the wolves represent all the fairy tale wolves, good or bad as needed. These days Mollie makes her wolves docile and full of carrots.

30

The boys want more action. As Mollie's stories become more peaceful, Barney, Fredrick, and William stir up excitement. Barney devises a new Peter Rabbit ending that displeases Mollie.

"One day Peter Rabbit's mother said, 'Don't go into Mr. McGregor's garden.' But Peter went under the gate. Then Mr. McGregor tried to catch him and he caught him and ate him for dinner."

"That's *not* what he did, Barney," Mollie says. "People don't eat rabbits."

"They do kill rabbits with their swords," Fredrick states

authoritatively and then goes even further in his own Peter Rabbit story. "Mr. McGregor gets Peter's mother. Then they fight with swords. Then Peter kicks Mr. McGregor in the face. Then they boom each other. Then Batman comes. Then the mother goes home."

William captures the new style in a single sentence: "Peter Rabbit cooks Mr. McGregor."

"Does he think he's a carrot?" Christopher asks.

"Yes, he thinks he's a carrot stew."

Upstairs, I preface the stories with a comment. "Barney, Fredrick, and William told Peter Rabbit stories that are quite interesting."

"Why? What's so interesting about that?" Erik is not in the mood for compliments directed to others. As always, his cynicism has the effect of focusing children's attention to the matter at hand.

'Well, in the book Peter runs home and is put to bed with camomile tea. But in these stories very different things happen."

After we act out the stories, Erik says, "Tomorrow I might do that." However, the next day it is again Barney who revises a well-known story. "The baby billy goat said, 'Wait for my big brother.' The troll didn't wait. He stepped on a D and ate up the billy goat."

"I don't like that," Mollie complains. "I don't want him to eat the billy goat."

"But Mollie," Barney capitulates, "he didn't eat him all the way up, so he popped right out and the good Darth Vader came and pushed the troll in the water."

"That's a quite interesting story, Barney," Mollie says, imitating my tone.

In the morning, Mollie tells her own billy goat story. "First came the baby billy goat. Then came the mama. Then came the daddy. The troll was gone away. No 'Who's walking over my bridge?' part. Then they went for a walk in the woods and then they ate blackberries and milk for supper."

Stuart, quietly pasting squares on a cardboard, is suddenly visited by a new image. "Mrs. Paley, I forgot something. There's a wolf in my story. You didn't put a wolf in."

"Which story was that, Stuart?"

"The three bears and Goldilocks, that one."

"I'm pretty sure you took that story home with you last week."

"But there has to be a wolf in it. Because he blows their house down. So Goldilocks won't go there anymore."

How inventive are these three-year-olds; their fantasies bounce around like sticky balls, picking up usable material along the way. Christopher, for example, is telling a Peter Rabbit story in which Peter is chased by an elephant, when Adam runs up with a complaint. "Teacher, Maria called me a caterpillar."

"Don't call him a caterpillar, Maria. His name is Adam."

Christopher continues his story. "Then a caterpillar comes. And he's friends with the elephant and the bunny rabbit. And his name is not Adam."

31

Mollie's riddles enter the domain of fantasy play as if, to understand the meaning of a riddle, she must act it out. Today's riddle emerges intact from the doll corner where she pretended to take a bath in the toy sink, squeezing in and out of the small space with great effort. "Help me, Christopher. Pull out the plug so I can get out. I have to put my pajamas on."

At snack time Mollie recreates the scene in riddle form. "You put a plug in it. You get in the bathtub, then you get out of the bathtub. You put your pajamas on, then you get into bed. Mine you have to guess. It's get into bed at night."

Barney understands Mollie's new kind of riddle immediately and follows with another that also describes an entire episode, played many times with sand and water on the back steps.

"Mine has steps. First you do something in the steps by the wall and then you mix the cement in a little place not in the big cement mixer and then fix the step because it's broken."

"Steps!" the children guess.

"No, it's *fix* the steps because it's broken."

Both children have taken a real event, examined it through the prism of play, and then abstracted the essence into the shape of a riddle. The fact that Barney can so accurately grasp Mollie's intentions makes me all the more curious when my own purposes go unrecognized on three successive days. The first such incident occurs at riddle time.

"It has two bumps and it's a valentine," Mollie says.

"Trick or treat," Christopher calls out.

"That's from another holiday, Christopher. Who remembers when we say 'trick or treat'?"

"I *was* trick or treat," Stuart recalls.

"When? On what holiday?"

"Not a holiday."

"On Sunday," Mollie answers.

"I was Batman."

"That's right, William. You *were* Batman on that day. And we had pumpkin cookies."

"Pumpkin cookies day."

"Easter bunnies."

"Do you remember Halloween?"

"I was at Halloween!"

"That's when we say 'trick or treat'," I remind the children.

"You could say bunnies, too," Mollie adds. "That's a good thing to say."

Is my question "On what holiday?" misleading? Why should I expect three-year-olds, who have celebrated so few holidays in their lifetimes, to remember the differences, or to think it matters?

The next day, another "easy" question of mine suffers

the same fate. Of the eight children at the snack table six ask for peanut butter and jelly on their crackers, one wants plain peanut butter, and one, plain jelly. My question: What did I make more of, peanut butter and jelly or plain peanut butter? The children stare at me blankly and no one answers.

"What I mean is, did more people ask for peanut butter and jelly or did more want plain peanut butter?" Silence. "I'll count the children who are eating peanut butter and jelly." I count to six. "And only Barney has peanut butter."

"Because Barney likes peanut butter," Mollie explains.

"Yes, but did I make more sandwiches that have both peanut butter and jelly?"

"Because we like peanut butter *and* jelly," Fredrick responds patiently.

My question has misfired again and this time I can imagine several possible reasons. Since everyone is eating peanut butter and/or jelly, the entire group is included in the peanut butter and jelly category. In addition, "more" could refer to those who asked for more than one sandwich. Perhaps the word "plain" is the stumbling block or they may think I want to know why they chose peanut butter with or without jelly.

Another possibility: peanut butter and jelly may be akin to Peter and the Wolf, in that the words are not easily separated. Thus, "peanut butter and jelly" also represents plain peanut butter or plain jelly.

The third incident in which I overestimate our shared experience occurs on my birthday.

"Today is a special day for me, so I brought chocolate cookies for our snack. Who can guess what my special day is called?"

"Because if we have crackers it won't be a special day," Mollie answers. She hears a different question, namely, why do we bring special cookies on a special day?

"It's on TV," Tulio says. *He* thinks I am asking where I found out about these cookies.

"I know, I know," John calls out. "Because it's already

after Christmas." John, at least, may be trying to figure out what holiday it is.

"Yes, it *is* after Christmas. My special day always comes after Christmas. I get presents from my family and they sing a special song for me."

"Jingle bells."

"Because you buyed cookies."

"Valentine's Day."

"It's my birthday," I finally admit.

"Why?" Christopher asks.

"Why is it my birthday? We all have birthdays. You brought cupcakes on your birthday, remember, Christopher? So I decided to bring a treat on my birthday."

"Trick or treat, right?" Mollie says.

In all three discussions I anticipate the obvious response, but the children do not follow my thinking. Perhaps at another time they might have accidentally linked their images to mine. Of one thing I am certain: had I put inquiries into dramatic form and given us roles to play, I would have been understood.

32

Nearly everything makes more sense in the doll corner. When Mollie and the girls pretend to have a valentine party, she cuts out a variety of shapes and gives them out as valentines to everyone. However, several days later, on the real Valentine's Day, she refuses to pass out her store-bought valentines.

This is the doll corner version of the holiday:

"Ding-dong. Ring-ring."

"Come in. Who is it?"

"Trick or treat valentine."

"Don't say trick or treat to our house. The baby is sleeping. Don't ring the bell."

"I'm making valentines for the baby. 'I love you.' This spells 'I love you.'"

"Let's marry ourselves."

"We're marrying each other."

"I'm the bride. Hi, Mommy. Let's get married."

"I have to be a valentine. Only girls can come."

"No boys are valentines."

"Only girls in the wedding. Teacher, can you write 'I love you' on my baby valentines? This is my valentine to get married and have a baby. This is Valentine's Day."

"Are you having a valentine party?" I ask.

"It's the baby's birthday valentine."

When Valentine's Day arrives Mollie is surprised that her picture valentines are meant to be given away.

"But, Mollie, that's why your mother bought them. You're supposed to give one to each child."

"No, it's for me," Mollie insists, starting to cry. "It says M-O-L-L-I-E."

"Mother wrote your name so the children will know they're from you."

She cries more vigorously. "I have to bring them home. My mommy said."

"Okay, Mollie. Let's put them back in the box."

Instantly, the tears stop. "I'm telling a valentine story and it has a monkey climbed a tree. Then he fell down on a cushion. Then another monkey came."

"Which is the part about Valentine's Day?"

"The part about the monkey climbed a tree." Mollie looks at her box of valentines, then at the table filled with lacy red hearts. Today's event is controlled by others; she can think only of a monkey climbing a tree.

The image of the doll corner valentine party suddenly fills my mind and I gather the children around me. "I have a valentine story for us to act out. Once upon a time there was a valentine family with a mother, father, sister, brother, and baby. They were all busy making valentines because it was Valentine's Day. 'We have to write "I love you" and give them to all the animals who ring our bell,' they said.

"Ring-ring. Who is it? It's the four bears. Good. Here's your valentines.

"Ring-ring. Who is it? It's the four squirrels. Oh, good. Here's your valentines.

"Ring-ring. Who is it? It's the four elephants. Oh, very good. Here's your valentines.

"Ring-ring. Who is it? It's the four rabbits. Oh, very, very good. Here's your valentines. And all you animals must bring your valentines to the baby's birthday valentine party."

Mollie jumps up. "Wait a minute. I'm the sister. I have to get my valentines. I'm supposed to give them to the animals."

Mollie has an entree into the holiday. Moments earlier she was an outsider, just as she was, in fact, to school itself during the first few weeks. She worked her way to an understanding of school through the same doll corner fantasies that now illuminate Valentine's Day. And I, the outsider to three-year-old thinking, am learning to listen at the doll corner doorway for the sounds of reality.

33

The continual cutting and coloring at the story table would seem to be ends in themselves, appearing more purposeful than doll corner play. Often, however, they are background for other kinds of pretending and social discourse.

"I'm making people things whatever they want to do with these things," Mollie says, folding strips of colored paper. "Here, Tulio. You can have all of these."

"It looks like a motor."

"It *is* a motor, Tulio. You're right if you say that."

Tulio directs his attention to another matter. "You're selfish, Erik," he says, scribbling hard on a piece of paper.

"So what! I'm going to John's house," Erik responds.
"I'm staying when it's dark."

"Don't tell me no more. You're selfish."

"I am not."

"Yes you are. Teacher, whoever don't let nobody see
their toys is selfish."

"What toy won't he let you see?"

"That motorcycle."

"And you can't see the man either," Erik tells him. "This
is the last day I'm bringing this. Tulio always hasta see it."

"Tulio thinks you're selfish if you don't let him see it."

"He's wrong. *He's* selfish."

"But Tulio let people see his Darth Vader yesterday."

"Not me he didn't."

"Because I knew you wouldn't let me see the motorcycle.
My daddy's getting me a real motorcycle, the kind that
could jump over a building."

"I'm getting one that could jump higher than that."

"He's talking rude to me, teacher."

"What's he saying, Tulio?"

"He's talking close to my face. And he's telling me he's
going to John's house. I don't want to hear about that stuff."

"Tulio, I made you something," Mollie says. "Look, this
is for you." Mollie gives Tulio a handful of folded strips.
"Now, do you feel better?"

"I'm strong, teacher," Tulio says. "Feel my muscle. I'm
stronger than a motorcycle man."

"Let me feel it," Mollie says, gently patting Tulio's arm.
"I'm big too, Tulio. I'm bigger, bigger like you. I'm not selfish, Tulio."

There is no response from Tulio, who is busy punching
holes in his picture, so Mollie turns to Margaret.

"You're selfish, Margaret."

"No, I'm not."

"You won't give me your scissors."

"I don't want to."

"You won't give me that red paper."

"Here it is."

"You're not selfish. Teacher, I told Margaret she's not selfish."

Mollie treats new words as she would an unfamiliar costume, to be worn tentatively until the appropriate dialogue is found for its use. She takes "selfish" into the doll corner where Libby is managing a sick baby, two doctors, and a nurse.

"Be quiet, Mollie. It's the doctor's office. Doctor, does she have a diet?"

"A blood crusher."

"Don't put her in the baby carrier, Mollie. That's not what you do in the doctor's office."

"You're selfish, Libby."

"Okay, you could do that. But don't wake up the baby."

"Are you my friend, Libby?"

"Yes. We have to leave. The doctor is busy. Put her hospital dress on, Barney."

"I have to go shooting people."

"No shooting in the doctor's office. You're the *doctor*, Barney! Nurse, is the baby all right?"

"The baby is still sick. Give her eight vitamins."

"Mom, I'm scared! Someone will steal the baby!"

"We're not playing that, Samantha. You could be a doctor, too. Give her some shots."

"We're not selfish, right, Libby?" Mollie asks.

"Nobody in a doctor's office is *ever* selfish."

Back at the story table Mollie figures out her own definition for "selfish" as she watches Erik and Maria vie for position.

"Why did you do that to me, Maria? She hit me right there, teacher." Erik holds up his hand dramatically.

"It was an accident. I was trying to get the top off the marker."

"You hit me where it hurted. If you asked me I would take it off easy."

"I'll make you a good A, Erik," Maria says, sweetly. "That's not a good A you made. It's too round."

"Can you spell 'Scott'?" Erik asks her.

"Sure."

"Can you spell 'fire engine'?"

"Sure."

"Can you spell my name?"

"Yes."

"Yeah? Spell it."

"I'm too busy."

"Teacher, don't tell Maria how to spell my real name. It's a secret."

"Do you mean a different name, not Erik?"

"My *real* name. Erik is my pretend name."

"Is he selfish, Maria?"

"Uh-uh, Mollie. He don't hafta tell his real name."

"Get off my lap," Erik jokes, grateful for Maria's support.

"Get off my legs," Maria responds.

"Get off my nose. Get off my head."

"What is your real name, Erik?" Mollie puts her ear next to his mouth, waiting to be told the secret.

"I don't have a real name. Bad guys don't have names."

"Whisper in my ear, Erik."

"Okay. Bad guys don't have names," he whispers.

"Is that a secret?"

"Yeah."

"You're not selfish to me, Erik, right?"

"Right."

"I'm not either selfish, Mollie," Amelia says. "You want me to make you a magic book?"

"How do you do that?"

"Here, look at mine. It's a book of magic spells. First you have to fold it and then you make magic colors."

"Make me one, Amelia."

"Here it goes. Like this and like this. Here's your magic book, Mollie."

"I have a magic book, Margaret."

"Can you make me one, Mollie?"

"Tell Amelia. She's not a selfish girl."

No one asks about the powers of the magic book; it is enough simply to call it "magic." Mollie carries the folded

97

paper in her pocket all morning. "Do you want to see my magic book?" she asks. The children examine the book and nod seriously. It feels good to pretend, even momentarily, a magic control over the unknown, not too different from learning to use a new word.

34

The line between fantasy and reality wavers back and forth, finding its clearest projection in the children's own imaginative play. The adult who attempts to enter these fantasies often ends up by distorting reality for the children. Such is the case with Barney's father, a visitor today.

"This is our spaceship, Daddy. We're going on the moon, you see. No one can come in. Only Stuart. Only Mollie and Margaret."

Mollie covers Margaret with a blanket. "You're our little child. Go to sleep in your moon bed, baby."

"Can I join you?" Mr. Gliddon asks.

"You could come in, Daddy."

"Are you on the moon yet?"

"Right now, Daddy. We just got on the moon."

"Say, there's a nice moon person," Mr. Gliddon says. "What's her name?"

"Mollie."

"Do you live on the moon, Mollie?"

"I don't. I live at home."

"Is your home on the moon?"

"No. I live down that other street."

"Is the street on the moon?"

"No. This isn't the moon. This is the blocks. I'm not on the moon. I'm making something else."

"I was only pretending, Mollie," Mr. Gliddon says softly. "I know you don't live on the moon."

Mollie blushes and turns away; it is too late to make amends. If a grownup actually thinks Mollie is a moon person she'd better leave.

"Mollie, wait. I was kidding. Look over here. Look out the window. Up in the sky. There's where the real moon is. I know you don't live up there. It's a thousand miles away."

Mollie stares at Mr. Gliddon, then looks at the sky. "I'm three already," she tells him.

"Hey, Mollie, bring the Pepsi bottles," Barney calls out. "We're thirsty. Your baby is thirsty."

Mollie runs into the doll corner and returns with her arms full of plastic milk bottles. "They only had 7-Up," she says. "I have to dress the baby. It's time for school."

"No, stay here, Mollie."

"I can't. There's no school on the moon," says Mollie, reestablishing the equilibrium in her own way.

Her predicament with Mr. Gliddon helps me interpret an incident later in the day when Christopher appears similarly disoriented. He reacts in a far more extreme manner, however, and is unable to recover.

He has joined an animated discussion of "Star Wars," shown the night before on television, and is surprised to discover that *his* experience has actually been shared by others.

"Did you see it?" Libby asks. "C3PO said, 'I had enough of you,' and then he walks away."

"Hey, Libby! Guess what? I saw that too! In my house!" Christopher exclaims. "Then R2D2 said, 'I don't care.'"

"C3PO said that," John corrects him.

"Oh, yeah. Then R2D2 gets shot, doesn't he, John?"

"Right. See, they were sandmen and they had a big truck and they had a sand horse and they were in the sand."

By now Christopher is jumping up and down. "And remember Darth Vader? Hey, remember that? Hey, teacher, teacher, that's in my story." He sits beside me and speaks rapidly. "I'm Darth Vader. R2D2 sees a buffalo."

"Call it a sand buffalo," John advises.

"Sand buffalo. Then he throws a rock at the sand buffalo.

99

And then R2D2 goes in the rocks and finds some strange eyes."

As Christopher finishes his story, Amelia sits next to him, waiting for her turn.

"You can't tell stories, Amelia," he warns.

"I can if I want to."

"No, not Star Wars."

"Christopher, your story is over. Hers will be a different one."

"No, she can't be in mine. I'm not in a different one!"

"We know that. Adam, you're next on the list."

"No! He can't tell my Star Wars!"

"Christopher, please. He's telling his own, not yours."

"I don't want him to. Tell him not to do it."

Christopher is stuck in a fixed position just as Mollie was on the moon. For both children the sudden change in perspective caused by the intrusion of outsiders produces confusion. Mollie is able to extricate herself by adapting to another fantasy – pretending to take the baby to school – whereas Christopher cannot find a dramatic outlet for his anxiety.

"I'm sorry, Christopher, but Adam is going to tell his story right now. You'll have to excuse us. Why don't you go and play in the blocks? Look, no one is using the little animals."

On the way to the window seat Christopher passes Mollie sitting alone inside a small structure. "Can I play with you, Mollie?"

"Not you, Christopher. Don't come in. I'm Supergirl. Don't come in!"

"Stop pushing me, Mollie!"

"*Don't* come in. Don't. You'll knock it down."

"I won't."

"Go away. Don't touch my house."

"You can't say that, Mollie."

"Yes I can."

"No you can't! Don't say bad things in my ear!"

"All right, Christopher. You can be Supermouse."

"No! I'm not playing with you, Mollie. You're not good to me."

He complains to Mrs. Alter. "Mollie is bad to me. I'm not playing with her."

"Wait until she acts nicer."

"I'm *not* waiting!" He collects the animals and heads for the window seat but this time he does not turn his back to the room. He pays closer attention to Mollie in her little enclave than to the animals lined up in front of him.

In the morning Christopher goes directly to the block area. "I'm building a house, Mollie. You could come in. You wanna come in?"

"Okay. I'll bring the clothes," she answers. "We need lotsa stuff and things."

The two cover themselves with piles of doll corner furnishings and pretend to sleep. When Margaret arrives she asks Mollie if she can come in, but it is Christopher who answers.

"Lie down here. We're sand buffaloes."

"No, Christopher. You're a tiny person and Margaret is a tiny person and I'm a big person and the big person becomes a tiny person."

"I'm a tiny sand buffalo. You could be my mother, Mollie."

"I don't want to be a sand buffalo, Christopher. I want to be a lady mother."

"This sand buffalo does have a lady mother."

"Okay, Christopher. That's a good idea."

It *is* a good idea, arrived at out of Christopher's need to continue playing with Mollie. For him to move from a given position, the incentives must be powerful. They are, in fact, the strongest ones a preschool classroom can offer: friendship and fantasy. Christopher is most likely to respond realistically to other children when they give or withhold these gifts.

35

The teacher's questions, bestowed as a gift, are not always received in the spirit of the giver.

"Mollie, why do you like to be the wolf so much?" I ask after one of her wolf stories.

"Because, because, you silly." Her uncharacteristic response is a sign of discomfort.

"But you do like to be the wolf, don't you?"

"You silly!"

What seems inappropriate about my question? Does Mollie imagine I think she is a real wolf? Or that I think *she* thinks she might somehow become a real wolf? Moments later Maria asks a similar question and receives a very different response.

"How come you *always* say, 'Let me be the wolf. Let me be the wolf'? Don't you never like something different, girl?"

"But I'm a friendly wolf, Maria. That's the kind you can pet. They're very nice to be."

The difference obviously lies in the questioner not the question. Maria wants to know why a girl would pretend to be a wolf since she herself never takes that role. Mollie is eager to tell her the advantages of being a wolf so that Maria will think well of her and give her friendly wolf parts in her stories.

My question is on a par with Mr. Gliddon's "Do you live on the moon?" Had Barney asked the question, Mollie would have understood immediately that the information was needed for character identification. Barney's father lacks clear-cut motivation; his viewpoint is obscure. So is mine.

The children cannot always figure out the adults' relation to fantasy play. What powers do we possess that might affect the outcome? Can we, for instance, hear the children's thoughts?

"Why is Leslie doing that?" Mollie asks me.

"Doing what?"

"Crying in my head. Did you listen?"

"Mollie, I can't hear the sounds in your head."

"Margaret, can you hear Leslie crying in my head?"

"Yeah, I hear her crying in your house."

"She wants milk from her mama, that's why."

"I already knew that."

I must have misread the question. Did Mollie want me to imagine that Leslie was crying? The children wonder about our literal approach to events. Can this worldly view cause a fantasy to disappear and, if it does vanish, what happens to the players?

Such is the concern when I unexpectedly appear at the door of the doll corner during a hospital drama.

"Come here, nurse," Libby says impatiently to Mollie. "Come here and undress the baby."

"Are you the mother?"

"Yes, and Peter is the doctor. I'm sick too. Hurry, put the medicine on me. I cut my knee. Put on the stitches, doctor. Look in my mouth. Say you see bumps. Put us in the X-ray."

"There's Mrs. Paley."

"What if she calls this the doll corner?"

"She can't see us. We're in the hospital. It's far away downtown."

"Sh! She'll think it's the doll corner."

"Get inside the hospital. We're getting far away so she doesn't know where the hospital is."

None of this dialogue confounds Mollie as did my question about her being a wolf, but the concept is the same: Do I understand the nature of the fantasy, and, if I don't, to what extent does the fantasy exist? When Mollie was two she did not see the discrepancy; by the time she is five she will comprehend both points of view. Right now it is sometimes a problem.

Mollie may wonder about *my* motives but never about Erik's. Later, in the block area, he is particularly unreasonable and yet he makes perfect sense to Mollie.

"Move it, Mollie! You made me trip!" Erik screams. "If you moved that I wouldn't have bumped my knee."

"But Erik, how *could* she move her building? You have to watch where you step."

"She always puts her house next to Maria. If that Mollie would get out of my way! I need to make a road."

"Mollie was here first, Erik."

Mollie steps out of her house. "You could be here first, Erik."

"Thanks," he responds graciously.

Mollie sits down at the table and begins to cut paper. I feel sorry about Mollie's easy acquiescence to Erik. "You know, Mollie, you don't have to leave the blocks just because Erik wants more space."

"Yes, because I'm making all kinds of shapes."

"Oh, there's a triangle."

"I made it for you, teacher. It's the top of a house."

"Then I'll paste it on this square and it will look just like a house, Mollie."

"Look, teacher. I made you a flower on the house."

"Water it then," Maria jokes.

"Okay," I respond in kind. "P-sh-sh. I'm watering your flower."

"You're funny, teacher. I like you," Mollie says. This sort of fantasy is acceptable from me. I am not stepping into an imagined world where Mollie herself has taken on another shape or dimension. Playing with paper shapes and crayoned flowers is quite different from the serious transformations in the doll corner and blocks.

Most of my questions, of course, are neutral, not concerning matters of fantasy but meant to elicit ideas and opinions about ordinary phenomena. I inquire, for example, about a picture of a large cat surrounded by baby bunnies.

"I wonder what the big cat is doing with the little bunnies," I ask.

"That's the grandma," Mollie replies. "They're visiting their grandma."

John has doubts. "Maybe she thought those were the cutest to buy for her babies."

"No, John, that's their mommy," Adam says. "She has to be their mommy. She lives with them."

"Can a cat be the mother of bunnies?" I ask.

"Sure, if she wants to she can," Adam answers.

"I think she's just taking care of the babies because their mother is at work," Erik decides.

Nonetheless, most of the children believe, along with Mollie and Adam, that the cat is either mother or grandmother to the bunnies. In the next turn of the conversation, however, the opposite view of genetics is upheld.

"The bunnies grow up to be sheep," Christopher says, seeing a picture of sheep on the next page.

Maria laughs. "No they don't. Bunnies never do that. They have to grow up to be big rabbits."

Everyone, including Mollie, seems now to agree with Maria.

"The baby bunny has to grow up to be a mommy rabbit," Mollie says. "If they think to be a sheep they can't."

36

Mollie has another new word. "My story is about something that's pretty *curious*," she says.

"What is the curious thing?" I ask.

"Not Curious George. Curious different curious. It's a wolf and a little girl are buying some gum."

"That *is* curious. It's unusual."

"Then some more curious wolfis come. Then they go home and eat supper. Tulio, is your story curious?"

"No. A cowboy comes and kicks Bo and Duke."

"That *is* a curious story, Tulio."

"Why?"

"Because it's Dukes of Hazzard. Tulio, can you build with me?"

"I'll do it later."

"Margaret, will you build a curious house with me?"

"I'm telling my story."

Mollie returns to the story table. Her new word gives her more pleasure if she can use it with others. She settles down with crayons and paper, ready to comment on Margaret's story.

"Once upon a time there was a sister who was a girl, and a monster came. And the brother got scared of the monster too and they ran home. But it was a nice monster."

"Teacher, Margaret is too curious. Tulio, will you build with me? Tulio, you're *too* curious. Tulio, I'm a curious wolf."

"Stop sayin' that, Mollie," Tulio scowls. "I'm never buildin' with you if you keep sayin' that."

Mollie gazes at Tulio with what could, in fact, be called curiosity. "Okay, I won't."

"Mollie, do you know how to dance?" Erik asks from the spaceship next to hers. "I mean rough dancing. I mean Michael Jackson. Teacher, do you know how 'Beat It' goes?"

"No, I don't."

Erik begins to sing "Beat It" and a number of children mouth the words along with him. "I can dance breakers to rough music. Watch me." Flushed and breathless, Erik flops about on the floor, knocking over blocks, causing a great deal of scrambling and jumping out of his way. "This is break dancing. Watch me do it."

The children are speechless with admiration. "Mollie," I whisper. "I think that's a curious way to dance."

"It's not curious," she informs me. "It's *real* dancing."

My use of "curious" confuses Mollie. All morning it has been her pretend label and suddenly I apply the word to a real event. Erik is not pretending to be Michael Jackson; he is Erik and he is really dancing. That is not curious.

37

"Remember when Erik was doing rough dancing?" Mollie asks me. "I'm going to show my mother how to do that."

Nothing I do or say arouses the same intense interest Mollie has in her classmates. After many years of teaching, I must admit that mine is not the primary voice in the classroom. Only rarely, for example, do my words find their way into the children's stories. I may draw attention to the storyteller's ideas, but I remain the commentator and not the inventor.

Barney is an inventor. The magic D was his and now he conceives of a key that opens bad people. The key is from one of his toys, a stuffed dog, and Barney makes it a symbol of power.

"Once there was a dog with a key. He went to Mr. McGregor's cottage. Mr. McGregor said, 'Stop, thief!' So the dog opened him up with the key."

"Opened the cottage, don't you mean?"

"No, opened Mr. McGregor."

When we act out his story, Barney reminds me, "Not the house. Just *he* gets opened." The hero must confront the antagonist in the most direct way. The key is an immediate success.

Mollie uses it in her next story. "About Little Red Riding Hood. Then her father came. Then the wolf came. Then her father opened him up with the key."

John tells an overcomplicated bad guy–good guy story and puts the key in, almost as an afterthought, to distinguish between the two characters. "The bad guy smacks the good guy because the bad guy thinks he's a good guy. So then the good guy thinks he's a bad guy because the bad guy thinks he's a bad guy. But then the bad guy is really the good guy and they have a fight and the bad guy wins. But he's really the good guy. The good guy is the one with the key."

"John, this is really hard to understand. Why not give them names so we know who is the good guy and the bad guy?"

"They don't have names. It's not too hard because it's me and Erik, and I have the key."

"I have a key, too," Christopher asserts. "My good guy has a key. It's a bad thing and it shoots bad guys. And then he turns back into Superman and he rides on a deer and he beez friends. And I'm the good guy. The bad guy thinks he's a good guy. And the good guy has a key."

This is the closest Christopher has come to reproducing someone else's story. The key as a symbol of authority makes sense, and the good guy–bad guy muddle makes even more sense. A good guy cannot always tell if he's good because someone might think he's bad. However, he may be really good but only acting bad.

The children follow the logic of these ideas better than I do. I would use a key in the conventional way, to open a door, not a person. And I require labels in order to tell good and bad guys apart. The children know you can't really separate good from bad because they are aware of being both at the same time; that is, they may do something called "good" all the while imagining something called "bad."

We are not pursued by the same monsters and we do not look for the same escape routes. This may be why I seldom spot a useful literary device when it comes along. For example, the juice drinking in Stuart's story:

"Once a little boy was walking in the forest and a wolf came. And a bear. A nice wolf and a nice bear. And they had juice to drink."

Suddenly, sitting down to drink juice is an official happy ending, even for Star Wars. "Luke Skywalker has to fight Darth Vader and Darth Vader has to fight Han Solo and Han Solo has to fight Sandman and then they all fight for a little while and a little while and when there is no more little while they can have juice."

You can risk a great deal of fighting if you know how to escape from traps by means of magic letters, open up bad guys with a key, and then sit down to drink juice with your adversaries.

38

This is Sybil's last day in our school. Her family is moving to Baltimore and for weeks she has talked about the house with "the basement to make noise in." Today she passes out chocolate chip cookies and chooses the book we will read and act out.

"Will I always be older than Sybil?" Erik asks.

"You'll always be a year older."

"I'm older too," Mollie insists.

"Uh-uh, Mollie," Maria says sharply. "You and Sybil is the same. You always hasta say you're bigger and you're older and you're everything."

"I *am* older. I'm not the same!" Mollie's eyes brim over.

"Mollie, you and Sybil are both three," I say as gently as I can.

"I'm already bigger!" Mollie says angrily. The children munch silently, watching Mollie.

"Come on, Mollie, don't spoil Sybil's party." I regret my words the moment they are out. Mollie is not spoiling anything; no one is disturbed by her outburst. The children look concerned and sympathetic, perhaps even a bit relieved that the tension of a farewell party has been rechanneled.

"I'm sorry I said you were spoiling the party, Mollie. It's not true."

"You told a lie, right?" Tulio says.

"I made a mistake. And when you make a mistake it's a good thing to tell people that you're wrong."

"I made a mistake, too," Barney says.

"Me too," say several others. Confession is as contagious as any other ceremony that seems to have the teacher's approval.

"The gingerbread boy in Sybil's book makes a much worse mistake," I say, holding up the book. "He believes the fox when the fox promises not to eat him. Sybil wants to be the gingerbread boy and John is the fox."

As I read the book, the children blurt out the plot. They have heard the story a dozen times, but act as if each new page harbors a secret.

"He's going to run out of the oven."

"He'll get away! The door is open, old man!"

"He's too fast because they're too old."

"Run, run, you can't catch me," Sybil cries, racing around in circles. "I'm too fast as can be."

"Watch out! He's tricking you!" Erik calls out as I turn to the page where the fox appears.

"Get on me, Sybil. I'll carry you across the river," John says.

"Are you going to eat me?"

"No I won't."

"He's tricking you, Sybil!"

"He'll eat you!"

"No he won't," Mollie says doubtfully. "He's only saying that."

"Come on top of my head so you won't get wet," John urges.

I raise the book to display the final double-page picture. "Suddenly the fox gobbled up the gingerbread boy."

"I told you the fox was lying," Erik says, looking around proudly.

"I don't want him to eat me," Sybil says.

"All right. I'll make up a new ending, just the way you people sometimes do. Let's see. The gingerbread boy jumped on a duck that was swimming by and the duck flew over the water and brought him back to the old man and the old woman. They hugged him and kissed him and made him a birthday party."

Later, Christopher takes the book to the window seat and examines the final page. "I'm in the water," he whispers to himself. "Swim, swim, swim, walk, walk, walk. Hey, Mollie.

Come here! You want to do this? Can I come on your back?"

"Okay. I'm the wolf."

"No eating. We beez friends."

Mollie stretches out to allow Christopher to sit on her. "And no troll under the bridge," she says as she begins to swim.

Sybil's departure is confusing. Every day at snack time the children tell me that Sybil is not here.

"She goes to another school now," I remind them.

"Why?"

"Because she moved to Baltimore. That's far away."

"Is she coming the next day?"

"No. She can't come any more. It's too far."

"Why?"

"Who will play with Carrie?" Mollie asks me. "Why don't you be Carrie's friend?"

"Me too, me too," they all say, but Carrie looks worried. Sybil had become her dependable, daily playmate and she feels abandoned. She didn't want to come to school today.

"You don't have a Care-Bear," Mollie chants, instigating a rhythmic teasing that moves from rung to rung around the climbing room.

"Ye-es-I-do-oo."

"Not any Strawberry 'jamas."

"Ye-es-I-do-oo."

"I ha-ave-Bat-man," Barney joins in.

"I ha-ave-Straw-berry."

"Batman is better, Mollie."

"I'm Fire Star. Fire Star is really really."

"Are there two Fire Stars?" Carrie asks.

"There *are* two Fire Stars. We're both Fire Star. You have to walk like this, Carrie. Put your hands like this."

"Me too! I'm Fire Star too!" Christopher cries, jumping from the top rung of the A-frame ladder and barely missing William.

"Stop that, Christopher!" I shout. "You can jump *only* from the second bar. You *know* that."

He scrambles to the top and jumps again, watching me. "No! Don't you do that, Christopher!"

"Yes!" He is back on top swaying precariously.

"Don't jump from there!"

"Yes, I will! I'm doing it!"

Before I can reach him he jumps off and runs around the room pushing into children and toppling crates and chairs.

"Sit here, next to me, Christopher. You can't run into people. Just sit down. I'm about to read a book."

"I don't want to."

"Yes, I want you to sit down and listen. You'll have to do as I say."

"Why?"

"Because I'm your teacher."

As I begin to read, my anger subsides enough to realize that this time Christopher did not collapse limply against me. He stood his ground and opposed me as well as he could. He behaved, in other words, in a more ordinary manner for someone feeling like a bad guy.

"Are you going to be good?" Mollie asks Christopher when the story is finished.

"Don't say that to me."

"Okay. Do you want to be the bad baby?" she suggests, offering him a more acceptable way to identify his feelings.

"A good baby."

"Then you're the good baby. This is the chimney. You have to be sick. Here's where the people are sick. I'm the doctor."

"And then I change into Superman."

"You're not the baby?"

"I turned into Superman." Christopher runs to the ladder and climbs quickly to the top. "Superman!" he yells. Then he looks in my direction, carefully lowers himself to the second rung, and jumps.

39

"Margaret's not my friend, Mrs. Paley," Mollie says the next morning.

"Why do you think that?"

"She said she's not my friend. She even told me."

"Is it because Carrie is the second Fire Star?"

"Yes."

Mollie informs Christopher the moment he arrives. "Margaret is not my friend."

"Oh," he says, not asking for reasons. "Am I your friend?"

"Yes, if you help me make a restaurant. Bring those big blocks before Margaret gets them."

"Fish and chips."

"Kentucky-fried. Hi, Margaret. Are you going to be my friend today?"

"Yes."

"Then do you want Chinese noodles?"

"Cheese regular."

"Margaret, you're coming to my birthday."

"Me too?" Christopher asks.

"You're coming too. And Carrie and Sybil can be whatever they want in my story. They can be Fire Star."

"I want to be Fire Star," Margaret pouts.

"There's one, two, three Fire Stars. A mother Fire Star and there is a sister Fire Star and another sister Fire Star."

"Fire Star can't go swimming in the ocean, Mollie," Erik calls out from the sand table. "Sharks will bite you. Only John and me can go because we have secret powers."

Christopher climbs over the restaurant wall and runs to the sand table. "Erik? Hey, Erik you know what?"

"Shut up."

"Erik?"

"Be quiet, Christopher. I don't want to hear your stupid voice."

"Erik?"

"I'm going to punch you if you say my name."

"Hold on, Erik. Why so unfriendly?" I ask. "Christopher wants to tell you something."

"I'm busy waiting for John."

"You can still wait for John. But let Christopher speak to you. What do you want to say, Christopher?"

"Erik? Can I play with you?"

"No way."

"Why can't he, Erik?"

"Because when I let him play he crawls all over me and sits on me and pulls my shirt and grabs my gun and he messes up my tunnel. And me and John want to play without this kid."

John rushes into the room. "Battle Cat! I got Battle Cat!"

"Look, John. A secret tunnel. The bad guy is under here. He's dead."

"Shut up, Erik. Shut up!" Christopher blurts out angrily. The boys turn in surprise to look at Christopher who is rolling a car around in the sand. "Just shut up, Erik! Don't talk to me. Just be quiet. Don't crawl all over me neither. Don't do anything to me!"

"Teacher! Christopher's being rude to me."

"Don't say my name, Erik. That's not even my name. And don't touch my secret tunnel," Christopher adds. "There's a bad guy in there."

"Can I see it?" Barney asks.

"Yeah, but not Erik."

"Who cares!" Somehow, Erik looks as if he does care.

40

"Look what I painted, Christopher," Mollie says. "Guess something that lives in the woods. Guess it's a turtle."

"A turtle."

"Right. Turtles have very kinds of colors. Green is their

favorite color. And red. And blue. Turtles have very, very colors."

"That ain't no turtle," Erik says.

"Yeah, it is too a turtle!" Maria states. "Maybe you never saw that kind."

"How old are you, Maria?" Mollie asks, admiringly.

"Five."

"Teacher, did you know Maria is five? Five is a big girl."

"Who cares!" Erik shouts. "My brother is twelve."

"Erik, you know what? When I'm four I'm going to be five just like Maria. Then I'll be just the same as Maria."

"Yeah, I know."

We all know that Mollie cares a great deal about Maria and the other big girls. After months of listening to their stories, Mollie foregoes her wolves and ghosts and turns to a subject of deeper current interest to them: mothers and daughters. Each girl seems to have a characteristic approach. Maria's heroines, for example, usually disobey their mothers, leave home, and are brought back by a superhero.

"Once there was a little girl that went out to play. Her mother called her name but she didn't come. She wanted to go and play but Spiderman took the little girl to his web house to live. Then Superman rescued her to back where she lived and she played all day with her mother and they drew pictures."

Libby's stories avoid all suspense. "There was a little girl named Sally. Then she went for a walk in the woods and she met a rabbit. Then her mother came. Sally and the mother and the baby rabbit picked flowers."

Samantha's little girl is regularly saved by her mother. "Once upon a time there was a little girl. She asked her mother could she go out and play and her mother said yes. And a monster came. And the monster was very fast and the monster was going to eat her but her mother said, 'Jump on your bike and pedal very fast.' The girl pedaled so fast the monster fell down and the mother covered him into a hole she was digging. Then they picked flowers and when they got home they made valentines."

None of the boys have their characters pick flowers or make valentines, but nearly all the girls do. Mollie has begun to fill her stories with these tranquil occupations as deliberately as the boys omit them.

"My story is about a little girl who goes to the park to see her mother. They play and play and drink and drink all the juice and all the play they can do. And then they pick flowers and color flowers and pick flowers and color flowers."

In this class all the girls draw and color more than any of the boys who, in turn, spend more time running and shouting "bang bang." Their stories accurately reflect these preferences in play.

Christopher would rather be with Mollie than anyone else, but he prefers Erik's stories and much of Erik's play. When Erik sits down to tell a story, Christopher squeezes between us and whispers the endings of every sentence. It is one of the rare instances in which Erik is patient with Christopher, as if sensing that he is passing on a cultural heritage to a younger boy.

"The Dukes of Hazzard are driving in the General Lee," Erik's story begins.

"In the General Lee" is the echo.

"Then Roscoe was chasing them and there was a big wall and Duke's car jumped over it, but Roscoe jumped and crashed into the wall. And the Dukes shoot the bad guys."

"Shoot the bad guys, shoot the bad guys," Christopher trails off. "Hey, I'm telling a Dukes' story, too. And the Dukes run and they get into a car. Then a big hungry thing comes. The deer is the hungry thing. The Dukes pull the deer's horns and push him down."

"Are you one of the Dukes?" I ask.

"I'm the deer. Erik and John are the Dukes."

"Why do they pull the deer's horns?"

"Because he butted into them and bended their car."

If only Christopher's hungry deer could join Stuart's gentle giraffe family who walk in the woods, eat leaves, and drink juice. But Christopher's deer must annoy the Dukes and be punished. However, even Stuart shows signs of changing his image, for he is not indifferent to the beckonings of his peers.

Stopping to watch Fredrick and Barney in the blocks, he finds he must identify himself as good guy or bad.

"Bad guy! A ski masker!" Fredrick shouts, pointing at Stuart.

Barney follows suit. "Bang! Bang! A bad guy. A ski masker!"

"I'm not a ski masker. I'm a good guy," Stuart declares.

"Calling for Stuart! Calling for Stuart! Bad guys are here!"

"I'm a good guy," Stuart repeats.

"Stick 'em up or I'll shoot you," Fredrick says.

"No, because I'm a policeman. I'll bang at the bad guys. Bang! Bang!"

"Don't bang me, Stuart," Mollie tells him. She is sitting in a spaceship a few feet away. "Hey, Stuart, you wanna be a witch in my spaceship?"

"Can I be Darth?"

"That's your blanket, Stuart," Mollie says. "Fix it like mine is."

"First I have to bang my gun."

"This isn't a gun. It's for the baby to hold."

"No, Mollie. I made it for a gun. Bang! Bang! See, it shoots real bullets."

"Don't shoot it, Stuart. You'll bother the baby. Now I have to dress the baby. We're going out for dinner."

"Aren't we witches? You said we're witches in the spaceship, Mollie."

"Right. This *is* the witch's house. You be the daddy witch, okay, Stuart? Let's take the baby to the witch's place."

"No, to the Star Wars place."

"Okay. First lie down. Here's your bed. Don't ring the alarm until we wake up."

"Don't forget. I'm Darth."

"I'm Fire Star. Did I tell you I'm Fire Star? That's not a

witch. Fire Star is a little girl who is a little girl *and* Fire Star."

"Who am I, Mollie?" Christopher asks from the window seat.

"Do you want to be a boy thing or a girl thing?"

"A boy thing."

"Then you're the Dukes. Put your bed here and be very quietly. The baby is sick. No noise."

Later Mollie puts her unique stamp on the mother-daughter connection: instead of saving the little girl, the mother enables the child to save herself.

"My story is about a little girl who goes to the park to see her mother. And a little boy wild thing comes. Then a monster comes. The girl was bleeding because the monster hit her. So her mother told her she was Fire Star. Fire Star fixed the monster on fire and the monster couldn't get out of the fire. Then the little boy wild thing was friends with all the friends they ate with. They all went to bed and sleeped."

Girls who start school as ghosts and wolves apparently do not settle too often for routine walks in the park. Mollie will continue to be "a little girl and a little girl who is Fire Star" during the remainder of the school year. She has found a way to express her feelings of growing bigger that is more real than numbers or birthdays.

"I'm tall, Maria. Look how tall I am. I'm getting taller. We're the same tall."

"Uh-uh, Mollie. I'm five and you're three."

"I'm taller, Maria. Every day I eat."

"I'm this tall, Mollie."

"I'm this tall, too. I'm five inches."

"No you're not."

Mollie is crying. "I'm already four inches bigger."

"Why are you crying, Mollie?" Christopher asks.

"Maria says I'm not too tall."

Christopher runs to Maria and pushes her. "He pushed me, teacher!" Maria shouts, surprised.

"She has to stay away from my teacher," Christopher says.

"I'm also Maria's teacher, Christopher. Don't push her."

"She can't be in my class."

"Maria *is* in your class. We're all in this class."

"I'm a big boy. I know how to swim."

"But don't be a big boy that pushes."

"Erik is a big boy that pushes."

"I'm Fire Star," Mollie says with deliberation. "I'm a little girl who is Fire Star. Fire Star is olderer than Erik. But not the real Erik."

41

The issue seems to be control: What does it look like, who has it, and how far can one's imagination carry it?

"This is a puppy house. Only for myself to play. Somebody can't help me 'cause I'm making a puppy house." Mollie sings to herself as she stacks the blocks. "Away-ee-oh-oh. Peter's going away-ee-oh-ee."

Maria arrives. "You wanna play, Maria? There's a puppy in here. It's a puppy house. No, leave that over there. That's for the puppy."

"You don't have to tell me, Mollie. I know what to do."

"I know what to do too. Not there, Maria. This way. Put it down over here."

"Like this?"

"That's the way." Mollie is pleased that she can so easily manage an older girl. She does not realize that older girls are often more agreeable with younger girls than with those of their own age.

"Mollie, you want to have a circus party? A real one?"

"Real with clowns in there?"

"I don't know." Maria is momentarily confused when Mollie appears to take "real" too literally. An older child would know she was pretending.

"Real clowns, Maria?"

"No clowns. Just the other stuff. I'm making tickets."

"No, let's be orderers. This is the Pizza Hut, Maria. A pizza circus party with those clowns and the honkers." When Mollie is in charge she knows if something is pretend, but she is uncertain about other people's powers. Can Maria bring a real circus with real clowns? A few days earlier Fredrick told the snack group that a horse lives in his apartment and the children believed him. Then Adam passed by and said Fredrick was lying, and Mollie was surprised.

"I can't play any more, Mollie," Maria says, noting Samantha's arrival.

"Oh, well, do your own stuff, Buck."

"It's not Buck, Mollie, it's Duff."

"Do your own stuff, Bluff. Do your own bluff, Pluff."

"That's not what I said, Mollie."

"You glump sump."

"Stop callin' me chicken names! Mollie's callin' me names, teacher."

"She's just making rhymes, Maria."

"I don't want her to."

"I won't say it. Can you play with me?"

"Not now, Mollie. I have to play with Samantha."

Mollie's eyes follow Maria in sad recognition that the limits of her influence have been reached. She sits quietly, making tickets.

"Can I have a ticket, Mollie?"

"It's a AB, Carrie. What color do you want?"

"Blue."

"Who else wants a AB?"

Erik examines the "AB," a paper on which Mollie has printed the letters A and B. "Me. I want one," he says.

"What color?"

"Green."

"Here's a green. Who wants a purple? Who wants a red AB?"

The children flock around Mollie getting their AB's. No one asks for the meaning of AB; it is enough to be included in Mollie's game. Soon Margaret and Carrie join Mollie and the cards begin to reflect the preferences of the new workers, namely M and C.

"Who wants a AB?" Margaret calls out, holding up an M. Christopher tapes it to his shirt and stands behind Erik and John, who are deep in dialogue. They are completing Castle Greyskull, the home of Prince Adam, alias He-Man.

"You be He-Man, Erik. I'm Skeletor, okay?"

"Say your guy shoots me, John. Ptu! Ptu! Say my guy hits your fire shooter and it hits your face but you don't die. Ptu! Ptu!"

"Wait, Erik. Say I shoot you and you're on top of Battle Cat and he's dead."

"He says, 'What happened?' Then he says, 'There's no time now.'"

"Yeah, get on top of Battle Cat."

Christopher pulls Erik's shirt. "Say it to me, Erik. Say to me, 'What happened?' Say it to me."

"Get out, Christopher. Look what you did! Watch out! Teacher! Get him out!"

Now is the time when the difference between Mollie and Christopher is most pronounced. She knows when to stop and he doesn't. He hangs on to Erik's arm with a firm grip. "Are you my friend, Erik?"

"No!"

"Yes, yes, you are. Come on. Be my friend."

"No! I'm not!"

"Yeah, say you are."

"Then I'm throwing you in the garbage. Stop touching me, Christopher! I hate you!"

"Erik, can't you just tell Christopher you'll be his friend?" I ask.

"I don't feel like it today."

"Well, Mollie *is* my friend today. My daddy is going to buy her a hundred pieces of gum. At my birthday."

Erik drops his angry pose. "Am I coming?"

"If you beez my friend."

"I'll play with you in two days. Here's a good thing. Tell

121

your dad I'll play with you in two days. He can get me the gum, okay?"

It does not take two days for the good thing to happen; in less than an hour, Erik and Christopher are standing together at my side. "Look, Mrs. Paley. Look! Watch Christopher. I give him my Spiderman and he gives it right back when I ask for it. He learned how to do that. I *showed* him how."

42

"Tomorrow we'll hide these," I say, filling baskets with candy eggs for the Easter egg hunt.

"Can we eat them?" Mollie asks.

"Sure. As soon as you find them. First you'll be a bunny and hide them, then you'll be a child and find them."

The silence at the snack table should forewarn me that I am overcomplicating the event.

"I'm a child. I want to find them."

"Me too. I'm a child, too."

"I know. But it's a game. You'll hide the eggs, then you'll find them and eat them."

"Except not the Easter bunny," Stuart says. A misunderstanding is brewing, but I decide to wait until the hunt for further explanations.

The next morning the class sits motionless around pretend bushes made of hollow blocks in which five bunnies are to hide eggs for five children to find. As soon as I count the first five bunnies, Mollie bursts into tears. It is not ordinary crying, but breathless sobbing.

"Mollie, what's wrong? You'll have your turn. We're going around the circle the way we always do." Her crying becomes more intense.

"Just go the other way, teacher. Then she'll be first."

Erik, who allows no one to gain an advantage, offers a plan that would place him in the last group to hunt for eggs.

"That's nice of you, Erik, but it doesn't seem fair. Lots of people want to be first, but the rule is they must wait for their turn."

"Yes, yes, do it! Do it!" Erik insists.

"Then you'll be last."

"I don't care. Do it! Do it!"

Everyone nods in agreement. "Okay, Mollie. The others want you to be first," I say.

The effect is magical. She lifts her head, smiling through her tears while she tries to catch her breath. I reverse the counting order. Mollie and four others will be the first bunnies but, before I can remind them that they are bunnies, not children, they begin to eat the eggs.

"Wait, don't eat them. You have to hide them." At my words, Mollie's tear-stained face appears ready to crumble, and the children leap to her aid. They surround her with hugs and murmurs. "Nice, Mollie. Don't cry, Mollie." Maria kisses her hair and whispers, "I like you, Mollie."

The easter egg hunt continues while Mollie licks her egg, the line between hiding and eating entirely blurred. Nonetheless, the children are pleased with the hunt.

Why did Erik come to Mollie's aid? The obvious answer is that he is a good guy who pretends to be a bad guy. He fulfills the other part of the role at dismissal time by nearly pushing Tulio off the porch bench. "I don't want him next to me," Erik whines.

"Sit here, Tulio, with Adam and me. Maybe Erik wants to sit alone." If Erik can sympathize with Mollie's unreasonable mood, I can do no less for him. Tulio doesn't appear to mind; perhaps he even imagines he is doing something nice for Erik.

My own thoughts remain with the aborted Easter egg hunt, a memorable example of how *not* to conduct business when in the company of three-year-olds. Had I deliberately planned for confusion there could be no better device than this assignment of roles based on numerical position instead of dramatic necessity, neglecting my own best advice: do as the children do; put it into a story and act it out.

We might have begun with a selfish giant (Erik?) who refuses to share his Easter egg bush, and a mother rabbit (Libby, for sure) warning him of the dire consequences of such badness. Add here a bevy of bunnies (Mollie included) who wave their magic wands to make the eggs disappear and, finally, the remorseful giant inviting one and all to a candy egg feast.

For this, Mollie would have gladly postponed her rewards; a three-year-old in possession of a magic wand exudes patience and understanding, and need not worry about the fair distribution of Easter eggs.

43

Stuart's father makes a brief visit to the class. He surveys his son's block structure with genuine surprise. "Hey, Stuart, that's really great. Remember the first time I visited, on your birthday? Your spaceship was so shaky it kept falling down."

"I'm a big boy now, Daddy." Stuart crawls out of his spaceship and comes to the story table. "I want to do my story with my daddy. Daddy comes in the story. Then Daddy and Stuart fight. Then they play. Then they fight again and again. Then Stuart says, 'Now play nice.'"

"What does the story mean?" Mr. Morris whispers. "We never fight at home. When I"m not here does he put me in his stories?"

"Never. But he does tell about big things – planes, trains, dinosaurs – and you're pretty big. In his story he controls you completely."

This would seem to be the message that comes across to Mollie. After Mr. Morris leaves, when the threes are in the climbing room, she deliberately provokes Stuart.

"You can't lift your leg like this, Stuart. You're too small."
With a grand flourish, he lifts his leg even higher than
Mollie's still outstretched limb.

"You can't do this, Stuart Morris!" She shifts her position
slightly.

"See, I can!"

"And you can't do this, either," Mollie continues, ignoring the fact that Stuart is imitating her every move. "You're
too little."

"Teacher, Mollie says I'm too little."

"You're just as big as Mollie and you're both three," I
respond, somewhat impatiently.

"I'm bigger bigger three. Three, three, three!"

"So am I!"

"I'm bigger four!"

"So am I."

"I'm moving to a new house and you're not!"

"I am too."

"I'm going to my grandma in Milwaukee and you're not!"

"Yes I am!" Exasperated, Stuart pushes Mollie, then
turns to me in confusion. "Mollie, see how you're upsetting
Stuart? You know he never pushes anyone. Now, look, I
think you're both bigger three-year-olds. You know why?"

"Why?"

"Because you never used to argue so much about being
bigger. Maybe people do that to see if everyone knows that
they're bigger."

Downstairs, the quarrel is forgotten. Or perhaps it is con-
sciously redirected, something Mollie is becoming adept at
doing.

"Hey, Stu, you wanna build with me, Stu?"

"Just us? No one else?"

"Okay, Stu, what should we *do*?" Mollie rhymes, giddy
with good feeling. "Stuart, I'm asking my mommy can you
come to my house every day. We're big fighters, right? Like
you and your daddy?"

"I'm making the food, Mollie. Bring in the food."

"Are you the daddy? These are the salad potatoes. That's

125

absolutely delicious! Now, you have to fix the roof. Daddies have to climb on the roof."

As soon as Stuart becomes Daddy, he is "bigger"; had he preferred to be the baby, he would be "smaller." In fantasy play you are as large as the requirements of the role you play. It is not size that matters, but only how creatively you play your part.

44

"This is a key chain when you try to open something when something is locked up and then you open it," Mollie tells Adam.

"So what!"

"So no one can look at this 'cause I don't want people to look at this because it might get locked and no one can look at this. It's a surprise 'cause I don't want anyone to look at this."

"So what! *I'm* getting a key *car*," Erik states.

Mollie is not discouraged. "Erik, you know why this is very delicate? Because somebody might break it if it's something that's delicate. Nobody can break my key chain."

"Who cares about that old key chain? I'm getting a key car."

"Erik, when your key car is stuck, this key chain opens up something if it's stuck. Does your key car have a door?"

"Yeah. Two doors."

"This key chain opens a door that's kind of really stuck. You want me to keep it for you? If your key car is stuck?"

"Can I keep it for myself, Mollie?"

Mollie shakes her head. "No. I can't put this key chain where it's lost. I'm putting it in my pocket. Roar! I'm a growly bear!"

"You are not, Mollie."

"I know, but I do have a key chain."

Before the morning is over, Mollie will have exerted control over most of the children in the class with her key chain. It is actually a chain with no keys, but she uses ingenuity, persistence, and good manners to turn the chain into a lengthy agenda for play.

"Don't make noise, Stuart. I'm with the baby."

"The bad guy is coming," Stuart says as Christopher enters.

"I'm a good guy."

"Here, good guy," Mollie says. "Lock the door with my key chain. Then no bad guys can come in."

"I'll lock the windows," Stuart says.

"Whoever is good can do it, but never if you're bad."

"Lock me up, Mollie," Barney says. "I'm a chain door."

"Where's your key hole?"

"Lock up my ears."

"Lock up my nose."

"Look out. There might be growly bears. Lock up the house so they can't eat the porridge," Mollie orders. "Everyone can lock something. Christopher can lock up the walls and Carrie can lock the floors and Emily can lock the beds."

"What can I lock?" Margaret asks. "I'll lock the sink and the table."

"What are you playing?" Libby asks.

"Lock the house up."

"What can I lock?"

"It's already locked up. I have to put away my key chain."

"You're selfish, Mollie," Libby says.

"My mommy told me to put my key chain away where it's not lost."

"You're very selfish."

"Here, you could lock up something, Libby."

"Okay, Mollie. You're not selfish."

Mollie scrutinizes Libby for a moment, then regains control. "You could lock up four things because you're four years old." However briefly, Mollie is still boss.

In the blocks, Tulio is equally persuasive, even without a key chain.

"I want to ask you something, Christopher," he says, taking a block from Christopher's building.

"No! That's my house!"

"Just let me show you something good . . . "

"No! Put it down, Tulio. No!"

"Christopher, look, I'm filling up the hole and then you'll have a doorway to your house."

"No! Put them back. I had those first."

Tulio changes his tactics. Quietly he says, "Hey, Christopher. Hey, you wanna . . . "

"No! Don't! Put it back!"

"But here's a good good idea. This is what *Erik* likes to do. How 'bout if we make a bigger house? Hey, just attach it there and I'll take a block and attach it there. Okay?"

Christopher takes a deep breath and examines Tulio's face as if trying to determine whether he is being tricked. "Yeah, Tulio. That's a great idea. And is this the door to your house? You come in mine and I come inside of yours?"

"And all the food goes down here. Put it down here, Christopher."

"Are you my friend, Tulio?"

"Yeah. But don't knock this down."

It is another giant step for Christopher. In permitting his property to be attached to Tulio's, he acknowledges the separation between the two and the supremacy of making connections.

"Can I unlock your house, boys?" Mollie says.

"We need it locked, Mollie," Tulio says. "I heard strange noises in the woods."

"All right. I'll lock up all your bricks so the wolf doesn't come down the chimney."

There is no arguing with Mollie's logic, but now Christopher feels he has something to lose if Mollie takes over. "Only let me do it, Mollie. It's *my* house and I'm sharing it with Tulio. So I have to lock up the chimney, not you. Because the wolf only barks at the person who builded the house."

Tulio and Mollie look at each other, and Mollie hands

over the chain. There is no arguing with Christopher's logic either.

45

Encouraged by his triumph in the blocks, Christopher is more assertive later in the doll corner.

"I won't give you any food if you're not good," Christopher threatens. He is the father and Stuart and Barney are his babies, crying and throwing off their blankets.

"I'm good," Stuart says.

"No, you're not. You're crying. Only good babies get food."

"I'm good. Put my pie on. My pie! My pie!"

"This is not what I'm cooking. The father says what's cooking."

"Give me what you're cooking."

"Only if you beez a good baby."

"We won't cry, Daddy."

"Wait till these are ready because they're too hot. But if the babies aren't good, no food."

"We're laughing."

"Okay. Here's some food, baby."

"I'm good, right?"

"Yeah, you're good now. Both of you get porridge that's just right."

Mollie enters. "No more food, father. No more food, babies. No more, no more."

"I'm finished now."

"You have to get in your bed. Daddy will cover you up."

Christopher cradles a doll in his arms and begins to sway dreamily in the rocking chair. "M-m-m, go to sleep, little baby doll, m-m-m." The bell rings for outdoor play and Christopher is alone for a moment in the doll corner. Then Emily comes to the door. "Are you staying in, Christopher?"

"I'm the mommy," he answers. "You wanna stay in with me?"

"Mommy, mommy." Emily gives Christopher a kiss.

"How about you be the daddy, Emily? And I'll be the mommy. And I can have a baby in my tummy. You can be the daddy, okay? It's morning-time, Daddy."

"I'm going to be the baby, okay, Christopher?"

"Okay, Then you have to crawl like this."

"I sleep. Babies have to sleep."

"Okay, Emily. I'm the mommy. It's nighttime. The mommy and daddy stay up late at nighttime. Who's the daddy?"

"I won't. I'm the baby."

"Maybe we can not have a daddy. Only a mother and a little baby. Hey, little baby, our daddy died. Your daddy died. I just got a newborn baby. That's you. You get to be a big daddy or a big mommy and grow up to be a boy. Okay, little baby. You want some blankets, little baby? You want to sit on the baby chair?"

"Da-da-da-da-da."

"Here's some dinner. We're having a tea party first."

"Okay, then I'll be the daddy, Christopher, because the daddy has to come home from work."

"You have to stay home, Daddy. I have to call up. Hello? Hello? I got paid to get the money. Bye-bye. I hope to see you another day."

"You go there. I'll stay with the baby."

"Who is the baby, Emily?"

"Not me. Not you."

"I'm the mommy, Emily. I'm still the mommy. Is the baby still in my tummy? See if you feel the baby kicking."

"Yes, he's in there playing."

"Let's have a little bit more hot tea. I'll pour the tea, Emily."

"First I have to call. Hello? My sister's in jail. Could you get her? She must be four. I didn't know what she did it because I always know what she does. Goodbye. Oh, I want to ask you a question to the police. Do you really know why our girl always does that? I don't know why she does it.

Because. Okay, I'm going to call my father. Father, Father! Oh, dear. Goodbye."

"Emily, we don't have a daddy. He almost died outside because he died last Thursday."

"I didn't know that. Too bad. Goodbye. Never mind, police. We have to have our tea."

Mollie and Margaret walk in, looking surprised. "Why didn't you come out, Emily?"

"Me and Christopher stayed in."

"Okay," Mollie says. "You be the baby and I'm the mother."

"No. *I'm* the mother," Christopher states.

"You can be the daddy. That's much nicer."

"No, Mollie. I'm already being the mother. You can be the daddy."

Mollie takes her coat off uncertainly, and stands looking out of the doll corner window.

"Or you could be the baby, Mollie."

"She could be the sister."

"Okay, I'll be the daddy," Mollie says.

"Hold this, Daddy." Christopher hands Mollie the ladle. "Guess what, Mollie? Before, the father died. Now you came alive."

"I'm going to make cookies. Christmas snow cookies. That's what my daddy really does make."

Christopher joins Mollie at the window and looks down at the children in the playground. He watches Erik and John on the jungle gym, then takes off his frilly bed jacket. "Hey, Mollie, you could be the mommy. I have to go outside. I have to tell Erik something."

"What?"

"I have to tell him if I can be Robin."

46

Erik and I are standing next to the slide when Christopher comes out. "Guess what, teacher. There was Erik staying in my house."

"A boy named Erik?"

"No, he's at school. He lost his ball. It was in my house."

"Christopher, do you mean you have Erik's ball in your house?"

"*Erik* was in my house."

"He took my ball home," Erik says. "I never been to his house."

"You have Erik's ball. Not Erik. Just his ball. Please bring it back to him tomorrow."

"Erik. Erik was in my house."

"No way. He didn't even *invite* me."

"Yes, it's you, Erik. It was Erik because I saw him."

"Christopher, you pretended Erik was there. That's okay. A lot of children pretend things like that. But really, it was Erik's *ball*.

"And Erik, too."

I cannot persuade Christopher to stop saying that Erik has been to his house. Is this misrepresentation of the facts so different from Mollie's at dismissal time when she insists that Margaret is coming to her house?

"You are, you are, you're coming to my house, Margaret. Yes you are."

"No, Mollie. I'm going to Grandma Pearl."

"No, to my house. My house."

"Teacher," Margaret says tearfully. "Mollie can't bring me to her house. I'm going to my grandma."

"Of course you are, Margaret. Mollie, why do you keep saying that?"

"Because I have nobody to play with today."

Aren't both Mollie and Christopher saying they wish certain events could take place, just as Fredrick might wish a horse lived in his apartment? Yet Mollie has good reason to think she can convince us since Margaret has been to her house several times, and Fredrick's fib has a chance of being believed because none of us has been to his house. Christopher, however, confronts the one person who is entitled to dispute his claim and does not see the natural limitations of his fantasy.

As if to demonstrate that anything Christopher does she can also do, Mollie changes her sister's name to Linda after hearing that Amelia's new baby sister will be called Linda.

"So is my baby sister Linda," Mollie says.

"O-oo! You're lying, Mollie!" Amelia says.

"I am not. My mommy told me her name is really Linda."

"Is she telling the truth, teacher?" Maria asks.

"Mrs. Nardick didn't tell me anything about it."

"But she *did* tell me," Mollie says.

47

"How old are you, Mollie?" Erik asks. We are all sitting on the porch enjoying the warm May sun.

"I'm almost four."

"Are you three?"

"I'm almost four."

"How *old* are you?"

"Four."

"Well, I'm four and three-quarters," Erik says.

"Ask me, Erik," Christopher begs. "Ask me that."

"How old are you?"

"Four on my cake."

"How old are you now?"

"Three."

"Who's older, teacher? Mollie or Christopher?"

"They're the same age."

"Mollie has to be older. She's four and he's three."

"Mollie calls herself four."

133

"Tell me the truth, Mollie, or you're never coming to my house. How old are you now?"

"Three."

"You could call yourself three-and-a-half, Mollie," I suggest.

"I'm three-and-a-half."

"Can I come to your birthday, Mollie?" Christopher asks.

"Everyone in this place can come, because everyone is my friend."

"Am I, Mollie?"

"You are, Christopher."

"Are you my friend?" Stuart asks.

"I am, Stuart. I'm the whole everyone's friend that I know their name." Mollie begins calling names. "Margaret, Carrie, Erik . . . "

Suddenly the porch is quiet, the children all waiting to be named. One by one, Mollie pronounces the names as if electing each child to a high post. She knows all the names, of course, yet each child seems surprised and pleased to be formally named and designated Mollie's friend. This is not the doll corner. This is real. If Mollie knows your name out here, on the porch, you are really her friend.

"You didn't say Samantha," Libby reminds her. Samantha is absent today. "And Sybil."

"Yeah, don't forget Sybil," Erik says. "Because a person is always in this class. Say if you go to Baltimore, then on another day you can come back."

"On your birthday," Mollie decides.

It is the last day of school. We are in the playground.

"Here's a new friend I found," Erik says, taking Mollie's hand. "She doesn't have a mother or a father."

John picks up the story line instantly. "Come in, lost girl. You want to come live with us?"

"Yes, because I'm lost," Mollie says softly.

"She's all alone. We have to take care of her."

"Sit down, lost girl. Are you hungry?"

"Here's your supper. Do you like noodles?"

"Here's your bed. You can live with us because your mommy and daddy are dead."

"Don't call her lost because we found her. Pretend we found her and she was lost. I'm her daddy and you're her . . . are you her mother?"

"I'm the high school boy. The one who takes her to school."

'I'll be the one who takes her to McDonalds."

"On her birthday?"

"She doesn't have a birthday because she was lost."

"We can give her one. Pretend it's today."

"Happy birthday, lost girl."

Mollie does not look lost. In fact, she has never appeared more certain of where she is, of who she is.

Epilogue

It is seven months later; Mollie is four. Maria, Erik, and the other "big" children are now in kindergarten, and Mollie's group is called "oldest." This snowy February morning they crowd into the block area in noisy camaraderie.

"I'm He-Man," Barney shouts. "You're Teela, Mollie, okay? Mollie, listen, Teela! She's Captain of the Guard!"

"You want a sword, Mollie?" Fredrick asks. "Tri-Klops just hasta needs one so Teela could have this one."

"But now I changed my mind, guys. I'm playing Rainbow Brite with Christopher."

"No fair, Mollie. You said you'd be Teela," Barney argues. "You're supposed to live in Castle Greyskull."

Mollie shakes her head. "No, I can't do that. Rainbow Brite never lives in Castle Greyskull."

"That's okay because Teela could change into Rainbow Brite. Come on, Mollie."

She smiles at Christopher and pats his head. "Good horsie, Starlite. You come ride with me. We're going across the rainbow bridge."

Had Mollie been in last year's older group, it is unlikely Erik and John would often have allowed Rainbow Brite to modulate their superhero play. But the new boy leaders, Barney and Fredrick, run a different show. They continually encourage Mollie to join them, and the plot in the block structures moves back and forth between Masters of the Universe and Rainbow Brite. The He-Man story itself is now interlaced with cleverly disguised doll corner characters (baby He-Man, baby Battle Cat, little brother Cringer); hideouts and traps are furnished with pillows and blankets nearly as often as armaments.

"Try to escape, Rainbow," Christopher says.

"This way, Starlite. Pretend this is the bridge. Don't push down the blocks, Christopher, or you can't be Starlite."

Mollie views Christopher more realistically this year. Though he is still her favorite boy, she is less likely to accommodate to his erratic behavior; she sees the larger picture now and feels more responsible for curricular content. As were Libby and Erik the year before, Mollie and Barney are this year's arbiters of the rules for dramatic play.

"I'm your horse, too, Mollie," Barney says.

"No, you're He-Man."

"But Mollie, don't you know He-Man changed into a horse? There's such a thing. There could be two Starlites."

"Me too," Stuart calls. "Zip-zip, I just changed."

"Zip-zip" is an invention of Stuart's from an early story in which he couldn't decide whether to be a boy or a mother. "Zip-zip," he had the boy say, turning around several times, "I changed into a mother. Zip-zip, now I'm a boy again."

Barney repeated "zip-zip" a few days later in the blocks as an excuse to curl up on the bunny pillow in Castle Greyskull. "Zip-zip, I'm baby He-Man." Soon many of the boys were using the device, having discovered a way to deal with the ambivalence that sometimes confounds their play. How much easier to solve such problems when they are viewed within a framework of social fantasy play, where the premises can be controlled, the rules agreed upon, and the outcome evaluated with some degree of objectivity. Is it not a metaphor for problem solving in general?

"All right, guys," Mollie announces. "You could all be my horsies. You're on the team. First is Christopher, then comes second is Barney and Stuart is third and Margaret is fourth and Fredrick is five-th. Okay, time for breakfast, horsies. Want me to feed you?"

The boys make slurping sounds around Mollie while she cups her hands for each one. "Now you all go run again, horsies. Be good horsies. Give me a ride, Starlite. And *don't* wrestle me."

Christopher moves in a stately manner through the blocks with Mollie straddling his back. "We're all being good friends," she says. "Okay, horsies. It's time for oatmeal and raisins. That's all, horsies. No more. I have to make valentines. Rainbow Brite has to make valentines." She jumps off Christopher's back and runs to the story table.

As she gathers her materials into a circular design, colored papers surrounded by crayons, scissors, paste, puncher, and markers, I suddenly remember the three-year-old Mollie who steadily watched the big girls before deciding what to make, much as Dana now stares at Mollie.

"Give me that red paper, Dana. I need lots and lots of red paper. I'm making valentines for my grandma. Teacher, the mailman has to give me all my valentines to my door like in my valentine book. He has to knock on my door."

"But, Mollie, don't you live on the third floor?" I ask.

"On the first floor. Up on top we live."

"At the top of all the stairs? Near the roof?"

"Yes, my building is an impartment."

"Mollie, the top is called the *third* floor. Why do you call it the first floor?"

"It *is* the first floor."

"Then what is the bottom floor called?"

"That's the . . . fourth floor."

"Here, let me draw you a picture of your building. This is the bottom, where the mailboxes are. This is the top, right under the roof. Point to your windows."

She puts her finger on the top row of windows. "Here is my window where I sleep."

Christopher stares closely at my sketch. "That's the third floor, Mollie," he says.

"No, Christopher. It's the first floor. Because don't you know my house only has one floor in it? It's already on the first floor. On the other floors they call it other people's houses. Not mine."

Christopher nods his head. "Oh, that's what you mean." Living in a three-story house himself, he sees Mollie's perspective clearly; she has all three floors on one floor, the first floor.

Her error surprises me. Mollie has become so competent in play, I automatically expect her to have gained equal certainty in other matters; to understand, for example, that the third floor she lives on is the same "third" she used to count Rainbow Brite's horses.

Margaret frowns at Mollie's growing pile of stars and valentines. The two girls are officially "best friends" this year, passionately attentive to one another's newest skills and creations. They often spend entire play periods at the story table filling envelopes with their graphic displays. Early this morning they practiced writing I LOVE YOU, but now Margaret is in a quarrelsome mood. Mollie has learned to wait out other children's storms without adding her own tears.

"You have too many stars, Mollie. Just see how much. See? You should let other people too have anything or else I won't let you see my bag. And I won't let you have anything. Ever!"

"I don't care."

"And I won't let you see my chapstick. Don't even ask me. Don't even ask me to be your friend."

"I don't care. I'm going to have Easter at my house, Margaret. I'm getting bunny chapsticks and strawberry chapsticks."

"You better share your stuff, Mollie, or I won't share my stuff with you."

Mollie's responses are barely audible, as if to take the edge off her warnings. "I'm not going to let you see my Rainbow Brite dress-up."

"Then I'm never coming to your house again. I'm only going to Emily's house. Not yours. Don't ever invite me. If you do, I'm not going to come." With this, she sticks out her tongue.

"Margaret, that's not nice to do that when you stick out your tongue. And you don't even have big pony tails like I do."

"Mollie, if you share your valentines and stars, I'll be your friend, okay?"

"Okay. Do you know when Easter is, Margaret? My sister doesn't know. Don't tell Leslie it's in the spring. I don't want her to know."

"Only me and you can know, right Mollie?"

"I'm making this lovely thing for you, Margaret. Will you be good?"

"I will be good. I promise I will."

Miss Barton, substituting for Mrs. Alter today, arrives late; it is her first appearance in our room since the day last year when Mollie kept asking me, "Why *is* she Miss Barton?"

"Do you remember me?" Mollie asks her. "Do you remember someone called Mollie? It's me."

"I do remember. Hello, Mollie. I'm Miss Barton."

"I know," Mollie states. "And this is Barney. This is Christopher. This is Dana."

"Hello, children. Dana, you weren't here last year, were you?"

"She doesn't talk."

"Oh, sure she does, Mollie. She's a big girl."

"She's not too big. She's only three. She's shy."

"How old are you, Mollie?"

"Four."

"You had a birthday not too long ago, didn't you?"

"October ninth. That's a long time ago, isn't it? And my five-year-old birthday is going to be a Rainbow Brite cake. I've got a lot of stars to take home. I'm going to my grandma's house. I'm giving her these stars. That's why I'm putting them in this envelope very neatly. It'll probably take me a whole week to get these stars in here."

"Hi, Chris," Miss Barton says. "Shall I make you some stars?"

Mollie looks up in surprise. "This is not Chris. He's Christopher and he already knows how to make stars. He can even cut out stars better than me, can't you, Christopher? But he sometimes gets into trouble."

"I'm making Rainbow Brite stars," Christopher tells Miss Barton. "You can call this girl Rainbow Brite. You could call her Mollie or Rainbow Brite. Come on, Rainbow Brite, I hear a sound in the doll corner. I think it's the good witch."

Christopher does still get into trouble, but he has learned the importance of friendship and knows it must be expressed in terms of shared dramatic play. He can initiate spontaneous play this year as easily as he dictates a story, and he is certain of the connection between the two. In yesterday's story he made Mollie the good witch, and his present reference is to remind Mollie that, since he put her into his story, she is his friend and ought to play with him.

"Okay, Starlite. Margaret, you can be Rainbow's kitty. Here kitty, kitty. It's enough playing now, kitty. Time for my horsie. Starlite horsie, come get your food now. Once more now. Time for bed now, horsie. Go to sleep."

"I tricked you, Rainbow Brite," Christopher says. "Lurky is coming! He's coming in the back of us. He might be scaring us!"

"Don't worry, Starlite. I put the magic trap under the door. Then we'll give him the poison drink. Don't touch this. It's the poison drink."

"It's poison mud."

"Meow, I'm afraid of Lurky."

"I'll keep you safe, little kitty. Because Rainbow Brite has powers."

"Yeah, but I got superpower, Mollie!" Christopher shouts, climbing onto the top of the stove. "I'm Super Starlite! Super Starlite! I never go to sleep to watch for bad guys. I kick at them with my hind legs!"

Barney and Fredrick run in, surrounding Christopher with grunts and growls. "Hey, we're He-Man!"

"All of you can be Starlite," Mollie says primly.

"Uh-uh. We're He-Man now. Christopher, we're not

going to be Starlite, okay? We're going to be Battle Cat and He-Man."

Mollie looks hurt. "I have to get on Starlite and all the other Starlites have to wait. C'mon, Starlite, we have to fly to the store. You have to put your wings on. Fly, Starlite, fly."

"We can't be Starlites," Christopher says, not too defiantly. "Right, Barney?"

"Right! Look how strong He-Man is. You're Battle Cat, Christopher. I'll get on your back, okay?"

Mollie frowns at the departing riders and, for a few moments, absentmindedly fingers the playdough. Then she walks quietly to the story table.

"Can I tell my story? It's a valentine story."

"Only if it's short, Mollie. I was just about to ring the bell."

"It is short. First comes Rainbow Brite. Then she rides on Starlite that doesn't have superpowers. Then the valentines comes to Rainbow Brite's birthday party and then they have Rainbow Brite spoons and Rainbow Brite forks and Rainbow Brite plates."

Each time Mollie says "Rainbow Brite" it is a magical invocation. "And also Rainbow Brite napkins and a Rainbow Brite cake. The cake is the happily ever part," she adds, smiling.

Now that Mollie is four, her games are more complicated. Last year, one of her favorites was a paper-cutting game in which she and Barney cut and passed a paper to each other until it was shredded, repeating the phrases "You take it. Oh good, now you take it."

Today, Mollie's game sounds more like an illustrated story. "Barney, could you get me a piece of paper? My bunny wants to hop on it after I make a long road."

"Can I be the other bunny?"

"Okay. You be the bunny that hops on one foot. It's a race and then he'll win. If someone gets to this little rectangle right there, they win."

"Do I get the prize?"

"You can have it next time. In one longer hour. Because this time your bunny hurt his foot."

The snacktime riddles have carried over from last year. Mollie and her friends have learned to withhold the answers, but the riddles retain their idiosyncratic flavor.

Christopher calls out the first riddle today.

"It's something dark purple in a red can."

"Apple juice."

"That's not purple. I said purple."

"Purple juice. Cranapple."

"No, it's Cranapple, the kind my mother buys."

"My turn," Mollie says. "Mine is something it cuts through everything."

"Scissors."

"A knife."

"No. A pointy mouse's tail."

"I don't know, Mollie," I say. "Can a mouse's tail cut through everything?"

"It's a Rainbow Brite mouse. It can even cut through a piece of cheese."

"I just remembered something, Mollie. Last year you always wanted to be Fire Star. Now you're Rainbow Brite. I wonder what you'll decide to be when you're five."

"But I'm still going to be four a very long time," she says. "It takes a long time when you're an older child."

It is almost time to go home. Mollie and Margaret are cleaning up in the doll corner while Dana watches.

"Margaret is the magic star fairy and I'm the magic flying star fairy," Mollie murmurs.

"Are you sisters?" Dana asks.

"We're not sisters. We're friends."

"Am I your friend?" Dana wants to know.

"Well, I'm Teela now. She's Captain of the Guards," Mollie tells her. "So quiet, because we're in the forest and the wild animals will search for us and come and eat us up, so be very quiet because we're going through the jungles."

"Are you my friend?" Dana persists.

"Run, run, run, or we'll never see you again!" Mollie shouts, but Dana will not be put off.

"Are we friends, Mollie?"

"Yes, if you follow the rules. I know the rules, Dana, so I'll tell you what they are if you want to be a star fairy."

"Okay," Dana responds softly. "I'll follow the rules."